T0096344

NOTTINGHAM FOREST
On This Day

NOTTINGHAM FOREST
On This Day

History, Facts & Figures from Every Day of the Year

PETE ATTAWAY

NOTTINGHAM FOREST
On This Day

History, Facts & Figures from Every Day of the Year

All statistics, facts and figures are correct as of 31st January 2013

Published By:
Pitch Publishing (Brighton) Ltd
A2 Yeoman Gate
Yeoman Way
Durrington
BN13 3QZ

Email: info@pitchpublishing.co.uk
Web: www.pitchpublishing.co.uk

First published 2011
Reprinted 2013

A catalogue record for this book is available from the British Library.

ISBN: 978-1-9054118-9-4

Typesetting and origination by Pitch Publishing. Printed in Great Britain.
Printed and bound in India by Replika Press Pvt. Ltd.

This book is dedicated to my children, Ben and Louise, whose existence gives more meaning to my own than anyone else.

ACKNOWLEDGEMENTS

There are several people I'd like to thank for their contribution to this volume. First and foremost is my wife Elaine, who fast became used to mountains of football books and programmes littering the house, and my children Ben and Louise for having to keep quiet 'cos Dad's writing again'. I'd also like to thank my friends Jack, Jennie, Andy and Kim, and Chris for their interest and for giving me other things to think about.

I'd like to thank the legend that is Kenny Burns for supplying his excellent foreword; Geoff Peabody at NFFC and Danny Downs at Kitbag; John Sumpter of JMS Photography for the photographs; and Dan and Paul at Pitch Publishing for their help with this project.

FOREWORD BY KENNY BURNS

It is a pleasure to write a foreword for Pete Attaway's *Nottingham Forest On This Day*. In my career as a professional football player, I was very privileged to play for such teams as Birmingham City, Nottingham Forest, Leeds United, Derby County and Barnsley. I was a 'team' player and represented my country (Scotland) 20 times. I played in midfield, attack and defence. The highlight of my career was receiving two European Cup medals with the greatest Nottingham Forest team ever! Receiving the Sportswriters' Player of the Year and the Midlands Player of the Year awards was also something special.

I've enjoyed every football match of my career, from non-league to playing to crowds of 100,000 people at Wembley, Barcelona and the Olympic Stadium. I just loved to play football. I was considered a 'hard-man' but I can honestly say that I never set out to hurt anyone. When it came to tackling an opponent I wouldn't be beaten. It showed I was doing my job, and it was part and parcel of the game at that time. Things are so very different in today's game.

On my first day at Nottingham Forest I arrived with a 'bad boy' reputation, but I was welcomed by Mr Brian Clough and Mr Peter Taylor. The experience of that day will live with me forever. As the team began to collect trophies the supporters were tremendous. For a club like Nottingham Forest to become European club champions for two years was truly unbelievable – all the players, including myself, were nothing special individually, but as a team we blossomed and became a formidable force. Mr Clough and Mr Taylor knew just how to get the best from the team – for example, on Friday nights before a Saturday match they would get all the players together in the bar for a few pints – just to help us relax of course – and it worked! We went out onto the pitch the next day as a team and everyone knew exactly what they had to do. That was the result of not just one man (Brian Clough) but also Peter Taylor. Together, they made Nottingham Forest the great club. European champions – twice!

INTRODUCTION

To employ a well-worn metaphor, the history of Nottingham Forest Football Club can be neatly described as a rollercoaster. Admittedly, this would be a fairground attraction with a mile of level track containing the odd slight bump, before a meteorical climb into outer space, a slight but steady decline for a few hundred yards, then a trouser-wetting plummet deep into the bowels of the Earth, culminating in a gentle climb back towards an acceptable level of slight success.

My volume, I hope, neatly covers every inch of this ride on a day-by-day basis, rather than concentrating on those heady days of the late 1970s and early 1980s, when the enigmatic legends of Mr Brian Clough and Mr Peter Taylor took a bunch of provincial no-hopers and moulded them into the best team in the country, and then for a couple of years the best team in Europe. Sure, there are plenty of mentions of the likes of John Robertson, Kenny Burns, Peter Shilton and Garry Birtles, alongside later legends such as Stuart Pearce and Des Walker, but there are considerable mentions too for those Forest heroes who existed in times BC (before Clough). You'll read about the 'Prince of the Inside Lefts', Grenville Morris, club stalwarts such as Jack Burkitt and Bobby McKinlay, and crowd-pleasers like Joe Baker and Duncan McKenzie.

After Clough, a whole succession of lesser men have taken the Forest hot-seat to make their own impacts on the club's history. Some, such as Frank Clark and Dave Bassett, have enjoyed a degree of success. Others, such as Joe Kinnear and Gary Megson, are perhaps best forgotten. Billy Davies showed that a return for Forest to the top flight was at least plausible. Now, under ex-England coach Steve McClaren, all Forest fans are hoping that the realisation of that dream becomes reality.

Come On You Reds!

Pete Attaway

NOTTINGHAM FOREST
On This Day

JANUARY

SUNDAY 1st JANUARY 1959

Legendary Forest behind-the-scenes man Ken Smales was promoted from assistant secretary to the post full-time in succession to Noel Watson, who moved upstairs. A former first-class right arm bowler for Yorkshire and Nottinghamshire, Ken would go on to serve the club in the secretarial capacity for over 35 years, contributing regularly to the club's matchday programme and producing two tomes on the club's history. Famously, it was his signature that was missing on the forms that prevented Ian Storey-Moore from joining Derby County from Forest in 1972, the winger instead finding himself transferred to Manchester United.

THURSDAY 1st JANUARY 2009

Nottingham Forest confirmed the appointment of William 'Billy' McIntosh Davies as the club's new manager in succession to the departed Colin Calderwood. After an unremarkable playing career with Rangers, Elfsborg (Sweden), St Mirren, Leicester City, Dunfermline and Motherwell, Davies had moved into management at Motherwell and almost took them to European football before a poor run in 2001 saw him sacked. Appointed as Preston North End boss in succession to Craig Brown at Deepdale, Davies nearly guided The Lilywhites into the Premier League twice, losing in the play-offs each time, eventually making it one step further with Derby County in 2007. A dismal run in the top flight saw Davies leave Pride Park in November 2007, and he remained out of work until his contentious appointment to the Forest hot-seat just over a year later.

SATURDAY 2nd JANUARY 1971

Scotland 'Scot' Gemmill was born to the Derby County midfielder Archie Gemmill in Paisley, Scotland. While his father was known as a speedy playmaker, Scot – who joined Forest straight from school in 1987 and was given his debut by Brian Clough in March 1991 – was a more thoughtful player whose vision helped unlock a defence or two but who was prone to losing interest once a few tasty tackles had gone his way. Scot formed a superb understanding with Teddy Sheringham in his first season and served Forest's midfield for almost a decade until contract issues saw him left out of the first-team picture and eventually transferred to Everton. Scot won 26 caps for his namesake country, scoring once.

SATURDAY 2nd JANUARY 1982

One of Brian Clough's worst ever FA Cup reversals saw his Forest side defeated 3-1 at the City Ground by Wrexham, who were at the time involved in a relegation battle at the wrong end of the Second Division. The game began well with Forest's Mark Proctor netting after two minutes, but Forest paid for not increasing their lead and just after the hour Steve Dowman equalised, then two quick goals by Mick Vinter and Dixie McNeill sent Forest tumbling out of the competition at their first hurdle. Clough was so incensed by this result that he ordered the entire first-team squad in for extra training and a hastily arranged friendly with Luton the following Monday, which Forest won 5-1.

FRIDAY 3rd JANUARY 1975

Allan Brown's tenure in the Forest hot-seat came to an end. After nearly guiding Forest to promotion from Division Two at the end of the 1973/74 season, Brown had seemingly wasted the £240,000 generated by the sale of Duncan McKenzie and, with Forest in mid-table and smarting from a home defeat by neighbours Notts County, the board told Brown to clear his desk. The timing of the move raised some eyebrows, coming a day before a home FA Cup third round tie against Tottenham, which Bill Anderson took charge of.

SATURDAY 3rd JANUARY 2009

With John Pemberton in temporary charge and appointee-in-waiting Billy Davies watching from the stands, lowly second-tier Forest took a trip to Eastlands to take on the 'Richest Club In The World', Manchester City. Expecting a horrible mauling, the men in red shirts found their opponents possessed little appetite for a fight and consequently took advantage. A slip-up by Micah Richards allowed in Nathan Tyson who beat Joe Hart with a marvellous dipping volley, then just before the break Matt Thornhill's misdirected shot fell nicely for Rob Earnshaw who doubled Forest's advantage. An expected second-half fight back never materialised and City were out when Dietmar Hamann's sloppy throw-in allowed sub Joe Garner the easy task of driving the ball home for a totally unexpected 3-0 victory.

SATURDAY 4th JANUARY 2003

A case of the one that got away, as promotion-chasing Forest were unluckily knocked out of the FA Cup at the third round stage by Premiership strugglers West Ham United. Marlon Harewood, who less than a year later would be playing at Upton Park in a claret and blue shirt, gave Forest the lead after a quarter of an hour following a trademark David James fumble, only for Jermain Defoe to equalise. Andy Reid put Forest ahead again, Joe Cole levelled again just past the hour, then Gary Breen fouled Harewood in the box for a penalty. The usually reliable David Johnson slotted the penalty wide and with seven minutes left Forest paid the price when Defoe jinked past Chris Doig and Michael Dawson for the winner. There was one final bit of drama, though – with three minutes to go Harewood bundled the ball home only for the goal to be disallowed.

SATURDAY 5th JANUARY 1957

At the tail end of 1956, Forest's reserves had defeated Goole Town in the Midland League. At the start of 1957, Town found themselves pitted against Forest's first XI as a reward for reaching the third round of the cup by defeating fellow non-leaguers Wigan Athletic and Third Division North side Workington. There was to be no fairytale for The Vikings, though, as Forest ran out comfortable 6-0 winners, mainly thanks to a hat-trick by Jimmy Barrett. The other Forest goalscorers that day were Tommy Wilson, Peter Higham and Eddie Baily.

TUESDAY 5th JANUARY 1999

Dave Bassett paid the price for basement-dwelling Forest having failed to win in the Premiership since the second game of the season – which had been over four months ago – by getting the boot. The sales of Colin Cooper and Kevin Campbell, both of whom had been instrumental in Forest's bounce-back promotion the previous term, had not helped Bassett's cause, nor had the dressing room disharmony caused by Pierre van Hooijdonk going on strike. Having failed to defeat fellow whipping boys Southampton in his final game in charge, Bassett was shown the door. Micky Adams was given the task of keeping the hot-seat warm before the impending arrival of Big Ron Atkinson.

SUNDAY 6th JANUARY 1974

1974 was largely a dreadful year, being one of power cuts and three-day weeks. In an effort to raise some extra revenue, Forest moved their FA Cup third round tie at home to Bristol Rovers to a Sunday – the first ever game played at the City Ground on the Sabbath. They were rewarded by a crowd of 23,456 – the highest of the season – who turned up to watch Forest progress thanks to a 4-3 victory achieved with goals by Duncan McKenzie (a brace), Sammy Chapman and a George Lyall penalty. Forest would go on to enjoy a spirited and unexpected cup run until hooliganism ruined it all (see March 6th).

MONDAY 6th JANUARY 1975

The day the brightest spell of Nottingham Forest's long history began, when the expected appointment of Brian Clough as the City Ground head honcho was confirmed. After his amazing success up the road at the Baseball Ground, Clough had endured a lacklustre spell at Brighton followed by an infamous 'what was he thinking?' 44-day reign at Leeds United, and had become something of a tainted prospect within footballing circles. But Forest were willing to give Clough another chance, and the charismatic, enigmatic Old Big 'Ed was appointed to kick the slumbering Forest back into life. Seventeen years and several tin-pots later, his appointment could of course be seen as nothing more than an unqualified success…

WEDNESDAY 7th JANUARY 1976

…although it wasn't always successful. A year and a day after his appointment, Clough took his Forest charges down to London Road for an FA Cup third round replay against Noel Cantwell's Peterborough United following a dismal goalless draw at the City Ground the previous New Year's Day Thursday. Forest were mid-table in the second flight at the time but were still expected to beat the Posh, who were in second place in the Third Division. Even the prospect of a fourth round tie at Manchester United failed to inspire Forest, who were dreadful as they fell to Jon Nixon's goal halfway through the first half. So no trip to Old Trafford. Speaking of which…

SUNDAY 7th JANUARY 1990

...Alex Ferguson was not always English football's most successful manager. Having taken charge of Manchester United in November 1986, Sir Alex's early years at Old Trafford had largely failed to inspire and a tricky third round FA Cup tie at the City Ground was just what the press needed to state the nonsense that Ferguson would be sacked should United – then 15th in the league, six places lower than Forest – fail. At it turned out United ran out winners thanks to a Mark Hughes cross headed in by Mark Robins. United survived a late Nigel Jemson disallowed goal to go through, and would eventually go on to win the trophy, beating Crystal Palace in a replay. Sir Alex would still be in charge at Old Trafford 20 years later.

SATURDAY 8th JANUARY 1949

A tale of three goalies in one game for Forest as they took on Liverpool in the third round of the FA Cup for the second season in succession. The reds of Nottingham were 2-0 up thanks to a Bill Jones own goal and Freddie Scott with 20 minutes to go when custodian Harry Walker was forced from the field injured. Tommy Johnson went in goal, Willie Fagan pulled a goal back, and then, in the final minute, Cyril Done equalised. In extra time Johnson was replaced by Bill Hullett who managed to keep Liverpool at bay until the end of time. Sadly, these heroics went to waste as Liverpool won the replay 4-0.

WEDNESDAY 8th JANUARY 1975

The Brian Clough revolution officially began with his first game in charge, the small matter of an FA Cup third round replay at White Hart Lane, Forest and Tottenham Hotspur having drawn four days previously at the City Ground. In a fiery contest, the inspired Reds were the better team by a measurable distance, and just after the half-hour mark Liam O'Kane floated a free kick into the Tottenham penalty box and journeyman striker Neil Martin rose above Terry Naylor to plant the ball firmly past Pat Jennings. The disappointing Spurs side – who were 17th in the top flight and had future Forest boss Joe Kinnear at right-back – tried to gain a foothold back into the match by kicking lumps out of Forest, with only Alfie Conn seemingly interested in playing football. It was to no avail as Forest held on to progress in a pleasing win to start Cloughie's reign.

MONDAY 9th JANUARY 1990

In a surprising development, striker Lee Chapman was allowed to leave for Second Division Leeds United for £400,000, re-joining his former Sheffield Wednesday boss Howard Wilkinson. Chapman had been signed from French club Niort in October 1988, going on to score 24 goals in 65 games before losing his place to the emerging Nigel Jemson. Chapman would win a championship medal with Leeds in 1991/92.

SATURDAY 9th JANUARY 1999

Between the reigns of Dave Bassett and Ron Atkinson at Forest, Micky Adams had a game as caretaker boss. Playing at his former club Coventry City, Adams tried a 5-4-1 formation with Pierre van Hooijdonk as the lone frontman and a debut for the previously unheard-of Chris Doig. It was not exactly a success – the Reds went down 4-0 thanks to a Darren Huckerby hat-trick and a goal from Paul Telfer.

SATURDAY 10th JANUARY 1959

Most Forest fans will tell you that Forest last won the FA Cup in 1959. What they won't tell you is that the club very nearly went out of the competition that year at the first hurdle and in embarrassing circumstances – to non-leaguers Tooting & Mitcham. On a frozen and rutted pitch Tooting took a two-goal lead thanks to Albert Grainger and Ted Murphy before Murphy's backpass was allowed into the net by the Tooting keeper. Billy Gray then equalised from the spot to spare Forest an ignoble defeat.

MONDAY 10th JANUARY 2005

A player that Brian Clough signed but never rated – Gary Megson – became the latest incumbent of the City Ground manager's office, and within weeks 99.9% of the Forest support didn't rate him either. Taking over a side in freefall from the second tier, Megson couldn't save the club from relegation, and left the club a year and a bit later under genuine threat of relegation to the fourth tier for the first time in their largely successful history.

SATURDAY 11th JANUARY 1986

Legendary left-winger John Robertson appeared in a Forest shirt for the 514th and final time as a sub against Tottenham. Born in Uddingston, Scotland, on the 20th of January 1953, 'Robbo' would – after a fitful few years mucking about half-heartedly in the centre of midfield – become possibly Forest's greatest ever player, once his precious talent had been recognised and properly channelled by Brian Clough. Reportedly scruffy and unfit, the talented but under-achieving Robertson was on the verge of being shown the door at Forest before Clough exploded through it. Probably the vital cog in the Forest machine of the late 1970s and early 1980s, Robertson will be forever remembered in Forest folklore for two key moments: his supply of the cross which enabled Trevor Francis to score in the 1979 European Cup final and scoring himself against Hamburg, enabling Forest to retain the European Cup a year later. Two pivotal moments, but Robertson's lengthy contribution to Forest's glory years cannot in any way be underestimated. Sadly, though, it was his shock defection to Peter Taylor's second division Derby County in 1983 which soured the relationship between Clough and Taylor so sorely that it never healed. Robertson was brought back 'home' in 1985 for 11 cameo appearances before his retirement and subsequent success as the Taylor to Martin O'Neill's Clough.

MONDAY 11th JANUARY 1999

Ron Atkinson was appointed to steer the sinking ship of Nottingham Forest away from relegation after Dave Bassett's reign. The former Kettering, Cambridge, West Brom, Manchester United, Atletico Madrid, Sheffield Wednesday, Aston Villa and Coventry City manager would bring in a host of new faces, including John Harkes, Carlton Palmer, Stale Stensaas, Hugo Porfirio and Richard Gough, but to no avail, as Forest would end the season rock bottom of the Premier League. If they hadn't had three wins at the end of the season, they would have suffered a record low points total. Sulky striker Pierre van Hooijdonk described Big Ron's time at Forest with the line 'I got the impression the side was being managed by Rowan Atkinson', to which Atkinson retaliated with 'his (van Hooijdonk) biggest talent was upsetting his team mates.'

SATURDAY 12th JANUARY 1990

Not a good day to be a penalty taker for Nottingham Forest. In a league game at home to Coventry, Forest were awarded a spot kick, only for Nigel Clough to fluff it. Thankfully, the referee blew his whistle for encroachment and the Reds got a second chance. Clough allows Stuart Pearce a go and the left-back's kick was saved by Steve Ogrizovic. Happily, Forest won the game 3-0.

SATURDAY 12th JANUARY 2002

Rejuvenated striker Stern John made what turned out to be his final appearance for the club in a 0-0 bore draw at home to Barnsley. John had scored 14 goals that season, and one more would have triggered a clause in his contract meaning extra payments to the MLS – indeed, if John ended the season on 20 goals it would have cost cash-strapped Forest £330,000 in bonus fees. Paul Hart was told he was no longer able to consider John for first-team duties, and the hitman was sold to Birmingham City.

WEDNESDAY 13th JANUARY 1960

Billy Walker paid York City £12,000 for their young striker Colin Addison. Despite not having reached 21, Addison was thrust straight into the first team for a debut at home to Cardiff a week later, and he kept his place throughout the early 1960s, averaging a goal every one-and-a-half games. He was sold to Arsenal at the start of the 1966/67 season, who signed him as a replacement for John Barnwell, the player who'd taken his place at Forest. Following a brief stint at Sheffield United, Addison moved into non-league football and helped Hereford United gain a place in the league and guide them to their famous 2-1 victory over Newcastle as player-manager in the 1972 FA Cup. Addison later enjoyed a varied managerial career, taking stints at Newport County, Derby County and West Bromwich Albion, as well as spells in Spain with Celta Vigo and Atletico Madrid.

MONDAY 13th JANUARY 1986

Forest's turn to be the victims of a bit of giant-killing – they tumbled out of the FA Cup 3-2 in a third round replay against Blackburn Rovers.

SATURDAY 14th JANUARY 2001

Two players made their league debuts for the club against Crystal Palace at the City Ground – one who cost a lot of money, and one who would go on to be sold for a lot of money. The former was David Johnson, who David Platt had just signed for a £3 million fee which, in truth, was far beyond what Forest could afford. The second was rising starlet Jermaine Jenas, who'd play less than 30 games for the club before being snapped up by Newcastle United for £5 million in February 2002.

SATURDAY 14th JANUARY 2006

£300,000 hitman Grant Holt made his debut against Oldham Athletic at the City Ground and scored the first in a 3-0 victory over the Latics after 25 minutes. Holt would go on to score 21 goals in 96 games for Forest before falling out with Colin Calderwood and moving to Shrewsbury Town for £175,000 in the summer of 2008. From then on the forward made steady progress up the leagues, moving to Norwich a year later and reaching the Premier League with the Canaries at the end of the 2010/11 season after scoring 21 goals in 45 games for them.

TUESDAY 15th JANUARY 1980

There was a shock for Forest fans when *The Sun* newspaper announced that their chairman, Stuart Dryden, had been jailed for six months for swindling the Post Office. Dryden, whose sub post-office is in Ruddington, Notts, was found guilty of giving the Post Office false information and gaining money by deception.

SATURDAY 15th JANUARY 2000

The Reds came out second best in a frantic match at Grimsby Town which saw two players sent off and assistant manager Dennis Booth ejected from Blundell Park. It was 2-2 when defender Jon Olav Hjelde clumsily brought down Lee Ashcroft, who had given Grimsby the lead from the spot. Six minutes later goalie Dave Beasant saw red for handling outside the area. Kevin Donovan put the Mariners 4-2 up with seven minutes to go and, although nine-man Forest pulled one back in the last minute through Alan Rogers, Grimsby held on for victory.

FOREST'S COMBATIVE CENTRE-FORWARD GRANT HOLT, WHO MADE HIS DEBUT FOR FOREST AGAINST OLDHAM ON 14TH JANUARY 2006

SATURDAY 16th JANUARY 1988

Tricky winger Gary Crosby, a £20,000 signing from Grantham Town, was handed his debut as a sub in a home game with Charlton Athletic which ended 2-2. Crosby was recommended to Forest by ex-player Martin O'Neill, his manager at Grantham. Crosby would spend seven years on Forest's right wing, before moving to Huddersfield in 1994. He eventually teamed up with former team-mate Nigel Clough at Burton Albion, moving with Clough to Derby County in 2009. Crosby's most infamous moment came when he headed the ball off the palm of Andy Dibble's hand to score one of the most outrageous goals in history (see March 3rd).

SATURDAY 17th JANUARY 1891

Clapton welcomed their FA Cup opponents Nottingham Forest for a first round tie at the Spotted Dog ground, and then 90 minutes later were very glad to see the back of them as the Reds handed out a 14-0 spanking. Clapton had four players out through injury and, aided by this, Forest went 2-0 up within the first two minutes, with strikes by Arthur Shaw and 'Sandy' Higgins. By half-time it was 5-0, and in the second half the Reds ran rampant, firing nine goals past goalie Sam Gillam. Higgins, who only made the game at the last minute due to illness, scored five, while Corinthian Tinsley Lindley, who'd only offered Forest his services should Higgins not make it but decided to play anyway, netted four. Arthur Shaw added another to his first-half strike, Neil McCallum added a brace of his own and 'Tich' Smith chipped in with one.

WEDNESDAY 17th JANUARY 1945

Ian Storey-Moore, the best-ever occupant of Forest's number 11 shirt not called John Robertson, was born in Ipswich. Discovered by Forest playing in Scunthorpe, Moore (as he preferred to be known) spent a decade as Forest's version of George Best. He was supremely talented and an adept goalscorer, and if it hadn't been for Sir Alf Ramsey's dislike of wingers he would have won more than the single England cap he attained. He was sold to Manchester United in 1972 (after an aborted sale to deadly rivals Derby County – he was even paraded at the Baseball Ground), just as Forest were dropping out of the top flight, but injury curtailed his career there and he retired from professional football in 1974.

TUESDAY 18th JANUARY 1976

Forest decided they quite liked playing at Villa Park as the Birmingham ground served as the neutral venue for the third attempt at establishing a winner in their FA Cup third round tie with Bristol Rovers. Forest hammered Rovers 6-0, with goals by Tony Woodcock (2), Ian Bowyer, Peter Withe, Viv Anderson and John O'Hare, this following two 1-1 draws at Nottingham and Bristol. 'Justice was well served as we must have missed 16 goals in the first two games,' said Brian Clough.

WEDNESDAY 18th JANUARY 1988

A player hitting four goals in a game usually makes the headlines, but unfortunately for Lee Chapman, he chose to achieve this feat in a game immediately after which his manager Brian Clough took a 'hands on' approach to crowd control. Forest beat Queens Park Rangers 5-2 to move into the semi-finals of the League Cup, with Chapman grabbing four of them, but as a few excited Forest supporters spilled onto the pitch after the game, a maddened Clough slapped two of them. Despite Clough meeting up with those he slapped the following day and exchanging handshakes and kisses, the FA charged him with bringing the game into disrepute.

SATURDAY 19th JANUARY 1985

A dinner arranged by the Midlands Sports Writers Association to celebrate Brian Clough's decade in charge at Nottingham Forest by presenting him with £200 worth of cut glass was cancelled when it was discovered that Clough had chosen to fly to Tenerife on holiday.

TUESDAY 19th JANUARY 1999

Ron Atkinson made his first permanent purchase as Forest manager when he snapped up his former Sheffield Wednesday midfielder Carlton Palmer from Southampton for £1.1 million.

MONDAY 20th JANUARY 1975

Forest's perennial caretaker manager, Bill Anderson, left the club following the appointment of Brian Clough. Anderson held the temporary reins at the club three times, having formerly been manager of Lincoln City for 15 years.

FRIDAY 20th JANUARY 1984

Brian Clough was rewarded for Forest's excellent progress in the 1983/84 season (with the club making a sustained if unlikely push for the title, sitting in third place) by signing an extension to his contract to keep him in the City Ground hot-seat until at least May 1986.

SATURDAY 21st JANUARY 1984

Forest's commanding centre-half, Wes Morgan, was born in Nottingham. Rejected by Notts County at the age of 15, Morgan fell back into local football until being given a second chance by Forest in 2001. He rampaged through the youth and reserve teams before being given his bow in an unfamiliar left-back position against Port Vale in August 2003. Once Des Walker had finally retired and Michael Dawson had been sold to Tottenham Hotspur, Morgan became a regular in the heart of Forest's defence, impressing with his strength, aerial ability and a dribbling ability not normally associated with rugged centre-halves. He suffered a slight dip in form and confidence during 2007/08, but recovered and had his best ever season in a red shirt in 2010/11, during which he played every minute of every game and was voted into the PFA Championship Team of the Season by his fellow professionals.

SATURDAY 22nd JANUARY 1971

Forest's lethal striker, Stan Collymore, was born in Stone, Staffordshire. As a boy, Stan supported Aston Villa (a team he would eventually play for) and played football for Penkridge Juniors before undertaking apprenticeships at Walsall and Wolverhampton Wanderers, who both passed on the chance to sign him. He drifted into non-league with Stafford Rangers before moving to Crystal Palace in December 1990, Southend United in the summer of 1992 and then Forest.

SATURDAY 22nd JANUARY 1977

A Fulham team containing Bobby Moore, George Best and Rodney Marsh came to the City Ground but became the latest victims of the beginnings of the rise of Nottingham Forest, as they were trounced 3-0. Forest left it late as all three goals came in the last seven minutes, through Larry Lloyd (83), Martin O'Neill (87) and Tony Woodcock (89).

WES MORGAN, THE REDS' LONG-SERVING CENTRE-HALF, WAS BORN ON 21ST JANUARY 1984

WEDNESDAY 23rd JANUARY 1985

Guy Moussi, Forest's defensive midfielder, was born in Bondy, France. Scouted by Forest's French former midfielder David Friio, Colin Calderwood signed Moussi from Angers in the summer of 2008. A tall defensive midfielder full of energy, Moussi proved to be an astute acquisition.

SATURDAY 24th JANUARY 1959

Nottingham Forest progressed one step further to their goal of an FA Cup final appearance by defeating Tooting & Mitcham 3-0 in a third round replay at the City Ground. The scorers for Forest were Roy Dwight, Stewart Imlach and Tommy Wilson.

TUESDAY 24th JANUARY 2006

Gary Megson signed Wolverhampton Wanderers midfielder Sammy Clingan for Forest for a nominal fee. A hard-working player, Clingan would provide the centre-back pairing at the club with an extra line of defence for two and a bit seasons, before turning down the offer of a new contract and moving to Norwich City in the summer of 2008.

SATURDAY 25th JANUARY 1947

Forest, then mid-table in the Second Division, enjoyed a little cup superiority as they dumped First Division high-fliers Manchester United out of the FA Cup at the third round stage. With Old Trafford still being rebuilt after the end of the war, the game was played at Maine Road in front of 58,641 spectators, and Forest took the lead after half an hour when a Frank Knight free kick was received by Freddie Scott, who crossed for Eddie Barks to finish. Forest doubled their advantage after 65 minutes – Scott was the provider again, passing to 'Sailor' Brown who set up Colin Lyman to smash the ball home. The Reds of Nottingham held on to dump the Red Devils of Manchester out of the competition. Forest themselves would go on to lose in the next round to Middlesbrough.

MONDAY 25th JANUARY 1982

Following an uncharacteristically half-hearted display at home to Notts County (a 0-2 loss), Brian Clough placed the talismanic John Robertson on the transfer list for an asking price of £600,000.

TUESDAY 26th JANUARY 2010

Forest put in their best performance of the season as they hammered Queens Park Rangers 5-0 at the City Ground. Goals by Rob Earnshaw (2), Dexter Blackstock (penalty), Chris Cohen and James Perch secured Forest a handsome victory, although a couple more goals would have sent Forest above automatic promotion rivals Newcastle United to the pinnacle of the Championship.

SATURDAY 27th JANUARY 1974

Top-flight Manchester City were made aware that Second Division Nottingham Forest possessed a remarkably talented forward called Duncan McKenzie within their ranks, as the youngster masterminded a comfortable Reds win at the City Ground in the fourth round of the FA Cup. A long cross-field run saw McKenzie set up Ian Bowyer for the first, then he scored the second himself with an audacious scissor-kick from a lofted Paul Richardson ball. A second mazy McKenzie dribble beat four players before teeing up Bowyer again. George Lyall sealed an unexpected 4-1 victory.

SUNDAY 27th JANUARY 2008

Colin Calderwood told midfielder Neil Lennon he was free to leave the City Ground. The vastly experienced midfielder, who seemed to spend more time in Glasgow with his family than in Nottingham with his employers, joined Wycombe Wanderers four days later.

SATURDAY 28th JANUARY 2007

Right-midfielder Nicky Southall made his final appearance for the club in a fourth round FA Cup tie at Chelsea, which Forest were lucky to only lose 3-0. A surprise signing at the age of 33 in 2004, Southall played some of the best football of his career at Forest before being allowed to rejoin Gillingham for the second time.

SATURDAY 29th JANUARY 1958

A record midweek home crowd of 46,455 went home unhappy from the City Ground as West Bromwich Albion hammered Forest 5-1 in an FA Cup fourth round replay, despite the Baggies being down to ten men for most of the game after England international Maurice Setters broke his leg after 27 minutes.

THURSDAY 29th JANUARY 1987

Forest's flying winger Franz Carr turned down the offer of a new, £400-a-week contract with the club on the orders of his dad.

SATURDAY 30th JANUARY 1969

Sheffield United prised holders Forest's fingers off the FA Cup, beating them 3-0 at Bramall Lane.

WEDNESDAY 30th JANUARY 1980

On-loan striker Charlie George, playing to persuade Brian Clough of his fitness to join Nottingham Forest as a replacement for Tony Woodcock, scored after nine minutes to hand his temporary side the advantage in the first leg of the European Super Cup against Barcelona. Forest largely dominated but, despite the promptings of George and Trevor Francis, the Reds were unable to add to their lead and took only a slender advantage to the second leg at the Camp Nou a week later. Forest: Shilton, Anderson, Gray, O'Neill, Lloyd, Burns, Francis, Bowyer, Birtles, George, Robertson.

SATURDAY 31st JANUARY 1903

Grenville Morris hit the target in a 2-2 draw at Blackburn Rovers and, in doing so, the 'Prince of the Inside-Lefts' scored in his eighth game in succession. The superlative Welsh striker would finish the 1903-04 season with 24 goals in 33 games.

SATURDAY 31st JANUARY 1903

One of the best strikers in Forest's pre-war history, Johnny Dent, was born in Spennymoor, County Durham. A £1,500 signing from Huddersfield Town in October 1929, Dent went on to net a century of goals for the club before retiring in 1937 and going on to serve in the RAF during World War II.

MONDAY 31st JANUARY 2011

Forest made a surprise acquisition on transfer deadline day, picking up Liverpool left-back Paul Konchesky on loan. This solved a gap in the left side of the defence following the end of Ryan Bertraud's loan from Chelsea.

NOTTINGHAM FOREST
On This Day

FEBRUARY

SATURDAY 1st FEBRUARY 1975

Brian Clough suffered his first defeat as Forest manager, a 2-0 loss at Boundary Park to Oldham Athletic. The two Alans, Young and Groves, did the damage with a goal in each half. This marked the start of an awful run for Cloughie's new charges, failing to win another game for two months.

SATURDAY 1st FEBRUARY 1992

A sign of the dark times ahead? Forest capitulated horribly to Dave Bassett's Sheffield United at the City Ground, going down 5-2 to a team just five places above the relegation zone. Paul Lake, Jim Gannon, Ian Bryson, Carl Bradshaw and Brian Deane scored for the Blades, with Keane and a Pearce penalty replying for the Reds. 'We could have had seven,' reckoned Bassett.

SATURDAY 2nd FEBRUARY 1957

A Forest side making serious noises about returning to the top flight for the first time since 1925 travelled to Port Vale and recorded a handsome 7-1 victory. Jim Barrett led the scoring with a hat-trick, Stewart Imlach scored twice and Tommy Wilson and Eddie Baily completed the rout.

SATURDAY 2nd FEBRUARY 2002

No-nonsense defender Tony Vaughan made his final appearance for the Reds in a 3-1 victory over Stockport. An uncompromising centre-half, Vaughan was rescued from Manchester City's reserves, ex-Reds boss Frank Clark having paid £1.35 million to buy him from Ipswich. Initially signed on loan, Vaughan impressed David Platt and the Forest support sufficiently to join permanently. Vaughan's at times reckless style meant it was always likely refs would be waving red cards at him, something Paul Hart failed to approve of. He was eventually sent to Motherwell.

MONDAY 3rd FEBRUARY 1986

Forest director Frank Allcock resigned over comments made by Brian Clough in the matchday programme claiming Mr Allcock was offering 7/1 against Forest winning a recent match against Manchester United.

THURSDAY 4th FEBRUARY 1892

A 'Burlesque Football Match' took place at the Trent Bridge Ground between Nottingham Forest and 'Press and Pantomine' in aid of local hospitals. Sadly, the result of the game is not recorded. A century later, Brian Clough provided his own 'Comedy XI' as the club tumbled horribly back into the second tier.

SATURDAY 4th FEBRUARY 2012

A sad shock for Forest fans and football when owner and former chairman Nigel Doughty is found dead at his Grantham home, at the too-young age of 54. Doughty had bank-rolled the club for many years, investing almost £100m of his personal fortune into Forest, albeit with mixed results. Life-long Forest fan Doughty had resigned as chairman in October 2011 following the resignation of Steve McClaren.

TUESDAY 5th FEBRUARY 1980

The Reds got their hands on their second piece of European silverware, defeating Spanish giants Barcelona over two legs in the Super Cup. Defending a 1-0 lead from the first leg at the City Ground, Forest were pegged back within half-an-hour of the return at the Camp Nou thanks to a Carlos Roberto penalty, but regained the lead just before half-time thanks to Kenny Burns. Forty-five minutes of steadfast defending before a hostile crowd approaching 80,000 in the second half saw Forest victorious. Team: Shilton, Anderson, Gray, McGovern, Lloyd, Burns, Francis (O'Neill), Bowles, Birtles, George, Robertson.

FRIDAY 5th FEBRUARY 1988

The Welsh Football Association officially offered Forest boss Brian Clough the job of managing their national side following the resignation of Mike England. Clough was keen on the job but the Forest board refused to allow him to take it, even on a part-time basis. Clough's dreams of becoming an international boss never came to fruition – he was famously turned down by England and was also refused permission to take on a role with Ireland.

SUNDAY 6th FEBRUARY 1994

There was a debut for Norwegian defender and midfielder Alf-Inge Håland in a pleasing 4-0 win over local rivals Leicester City. Håland was the subject of a protracted transfer chase by Forest, taking nearly a year for the necessary work permit to be received. The blonde Scandinavian was one of the few bright sparks as Forest sunk back to the second tier in 1996/97, and was subsequently sold to Leeds United. His career was famously ended in 2001 by a foul by ex-Red Roy Keane in a Manchester derby (Håland having moved on to Man City) in retaliation for an incident three-and-a-half years earlier. Keane's autobiographical admission to the offence earned him a five game ban and a £150,000 fine.

SATURDAY 6th FEBRUARY 1999

One of the most appalling and embarrassing days in Forest's history. Manchester United came to the City Ground to take on the recently-appointed Ron Atkinson's new club and headed home happy with an 8-1 victory. Dwight Yorke gave United the lead after two minutes, only for Alan Rogers to equalise after six. This was the last sniff Forest had of goal as Alex Ferguson's class-laden team started playing (and scoring) for fun. Forest were 4-1 down (Yorke again and two from Andy Cole) with ten minutes to go when sub Ole Gunnar Solskjær came on, and he set a record for a substitute by scoring four times. The scoreline just beats the previous record for an away win in the Premiership, a 7-1 defeat of Sheffield Wednesday enjoyed by Forest themselves. Afterwards, Big Ron joked his team had given the fans a 'nine-goal thriller', but no Forest supporters were laughing.

SATURDAY 7th FEBRUARY 2004

Paul Hart was sacked as Forest manager following a 1-0 home defeat to Coventry City which left the club in the relegation zone. Having successfully guided Forest to the play-offs in 2003/04, Hart seemed to lose his way, not helped by the loss of demon strike pairing Marlon Harewood (for £500,000 to West Ham) and David Johnson (injury). At the time of his sacking, Forest had not won since October and hadn't scored a league goal for two months.

BRITAIN'S FIRST £1M POUND PLAYER, TREVOR FRANCIS, WHO COMPLETED HIS RECORD MOVE FROM BIRMINGHAM TO FOREST ON 9TH FEBRUARY 1979

SATURDAY 8th FEBRUARY 1958

A debut for South African goalkeeper Arthur Lightening was unusual in that he replaced another South African – amateur Harry Sharratt – in the Forest goal, Sharratt himself having been called in as emergency cover for the injured 'Chic' Thomson. Arthur served as back-up to Thomson until he was sold to Coventry City in 1959, where he became their regular custodian. A transfer to Middlesbrough followed in 1962, before he requested permission to attend his brother's wedding in his homeland in 1963 and never returned.

WEDNESDAY 8th FEBRUARY 1984

A fine win for Forest, beating West Bromwich Albion 5-0 at The Hawthorns with goals from Colin Walsh (penalty), Ken McNaught (own goal), Ian Bowyer, Garry Birtles and Viv Anderson. Unusually, Forest played the game in a kit of red shirts and dark blue shorts because their kit man had been unaware the Baggies played in white shorts. As Forest had only brought white shorts themselves, a set had to be borrowed from Albion.

THURSDAY 9th FEBRUARY 1957

The rampant Reds recorded their second successive 7-1 win, following up the massacre of Port Vale with another lop-sided result against Barnsley at the City Ground. The game was a personal triumph for young striker Tommy Wilson, who netted four goals. The other scorers were Peter Higham, Jim Barrett and Stewart Imlach. This result boded well for the forthcoming FA Cup fifth-round tie a week hence, the opponents being … Barnsley!

THURSDAY 9th FEBRUARY 1979

The protracted million-pound-plus transfer of Trevor Francis from Birmingham City was finally completed, although the actual fee Forest paid was £975,000 (taxes and other fees moved the entire deal closer to £1,180,000). The transfer eclipsed the previous highest deal, set barely a month previously when David Mills moved from Middlesbrough to West Bromwich Albion for £516,000. Francis was welcomed into the Forest fold with Clough's advice: 'Don't worry about what to do, just give the ball to John Robertson and he'll do the rest. He's a better player than you.'

THURSDAY 9th FEBRUARY 1989

Brian Clough was fined £5,000 and banned from the touchline until the end of the season for a mad fisticuffs moment in the Littlewoods Cup victory against Queens Park Rangers.

MONDAY 10th FEBRUARY 1975

One of the longest cup ties in both clubs' histories came to an end when Fulham defeated Forest 2-1 at the City Ground in the fourth round of the FA Cup at the fourth time of asking. This followed results of 0-0 (at Fulham), 1-1 (at Forest) and 1-1 again (at Fulham). The recently-appointed Brian Clough had now seen his new team play nine times in little over a month. Fulham would go all the way to the final where they would lose 2-0 at Wembley to West Ham United.

TUESDAY 10th FEBRUARY 2004

Joe Kinnear was appointed Forest manager in succession to Paul Hart. Having been out of work since May 2003 after being sacked by Luton Town, Kinnear's appointment was greeted with muted enthusiasm, but a decent run of results (P17 W8 D7 L2) was a significant improvement and the club hauled itself up from the relegation places for a decent 14th place finish. Phase I of Kinnear's task was completed in saving Forest from relegation, and with Phase II about to begin – Kinnear promised 'sexy signings' and chief exec Mark Arthur declared the club to be 'serious about promotion', what could possibly go wrong?

WEDNESDAY 11th FEBRUARY 1981

Forest took a trip to Japan right in the middle of their domestic season to take on Uruguay's Nacional Montevideo in the Toyota Cup, a rebranded version of the World Club Championship between the winners of the European Cup and the South American equivalent, the Copa Libertadores. Played at the National Stadium in Tokyo as a one-off game, Forest performed well but lost to an early Waldemar Victorino goal. Forest: Shilton, Anderson, F Gray, S Gray, Lloyd, Burns, O'Neill, Ponte (Ward), Francis, Wallace, Robertson. It was only Stuart Gray's second ever appearance in a Forest shirt.

SATURDAY 12th FEBRUARY 1955

A local derby at Meadow Lane against Notts County (and sadly a 4-1 loss), and a final appearance in a Reds shirt for legendary centre forward Walter 'Wally' Ardron. Previously with Denaby United, Wally was signed from Rotherham United in 1949, where he'd already made his mark as a lethal striker. He was handed the number nine shirt and responded magnificently, scoring 25 goals in his first season, then setting a still-to-be-beaten club record of 36 in 45 games in the Third Division South promotion campaign of 1950/51. Ardron was a fearless header of the ball, feeding on the accurate crosses supplied by Freddie Scott and Colin Collindridge. In total Wally would score 123 goals in 183 games during his time at Forest, to end with career totals of 217 goals in 305 matches – figures which would surely have been much greater if World War II hadn't forced him to delay the start of his professional career until he was 27. He passed away in 1978.

TUESDAY 12th FEBRUARY 1980

Forest ground out a 1-1 draw at Anfield in the second leg of the League Cup semi-final against Liverpool, winning 2-1 on aggregate to reach the final for the third year in succession. Having won the first leg 1-0 thanks to a last minute John Robertson penalty, a second penalty awarded halfway through the first half, when Ray Clemence felled Martin O'Neill in the penalty area, gave Forest a huge advantage. The Lloyd-Burns defensive combo stood firm against a Reds barrage, and Forest looked set for a rare win at Anfield until David Fairclough's 89th minute equaliser. They still progressed to another trip to Wembley and a chance for a hat-trick of League Cup wins. Their opponents in the final would be Wolverhampton Wanderers, who came from behind to beat Swindon Town in the other semi-final.

MONDAY 13th FEBRUARY 1871

Dennis 'Dan' Watkin Allsopp, Forest's goalkeeper in their successful 1898 FA Cup victory over Derby County, was born. A huge man, the Derby-born custodian joined Forest from Derby Junction in 1892, succeeding Bill Brown between the posts for the Garibaldis. Dan remained Forest's first-choice keeper until 1899, and passed away in 1921.

MONDAY 13th FEBRUARY 1978

A huge indication of how Forest had progressed under the stewardship of Brian Clough when Ally MacLeod announced his Scotland squad for the forthcoming friendly with Bulgaria. Three Forest players were in it – Kenny Burns, Archie Gemmill and John Robertson. Only Gemmill would play in the game, though, bizarrely preferred on the left wing to his team-mate Robertson. Gemmill captained the side and scored a 43rd minute penalty in a 2-1 win (the other goal came from future Red Ian Wallace).

SATURDAY 14th FEBRUARY 2004

Joe Kinnear's first game in charge of Forest was a fractious affair at the City Ground, with Walsall the visitors. It took three minutes for a two-month goalscoring duck to be broken, debutant Andy Impey netting. Jorge Leitao levelled two minutes later, Jamie Lawrence made it 2-1 when Darren Ward failed to hold Gary Birch's shot, and Gary Wales, who had set up Leitao's goal, curled the ball home for a 3-1 lead. Eoin Jess and Gareth Taylor were brought on at half-time for Gareth Williams and the on-loan Michael Chopra, moves that began to pay swift dividends as Forest staged a fight back. Just before the hour Marlon King pulled one back from an Andy Reid cross, then at the death Taylor headed Alan Rogers' cross past Jimmy Walker.

SATURDAY 15th FEBRUARY 1902

Forest's line-up at home to Sunderland for a league game had an odd look about it – reserve goalkeeper Alex Newbigging played at inside-right! Despite giving a decent account of himself, Newbigging was never asked to play outfield again. Forest won the game 2-1, with goals by Matthew Broughton and George Henderson.

SATURDAY 15th FEBRUARY 1936

The Reds took the long journey down to The Dell to take on Southampton, returning to Nottingham in a very poor mood after a 7-2 defeat. Southampton had two hat-trick heroes that day – ex-England international and West Ham legend Vic Watson, and cricketer Arthur Holt. It was the first time two Saints players had scored hat-tricks in the same match.

SATURDAY 15th FEBRUARY 1997

The momentum gained by Stuart Pearce's appointment as caretaker boss at Forest was well and truly extinguished by a 1-0 defeat at Chesterfield in the fifth round of the FA Cup. Forest were second-best to the third tier side throughout, and lost when Mark Crossley was sent off for tripping the dangerous Kevin Davies in the area. Tom Davies converted the penalty past sub Alan Fettis, and Chesterfield went on to nearly reach the final, beating Wrexham in the quarter-final and establishing a 2-0 lead against Middlesbrough in the semi-final at Old Trafford before eventually drawing the game 3-3 and losing the replay 3-0.

THURSDAY 16th FEBRUARY 2006

Gary Megson left his post as manager of Nottingham Forest 'by mutual consent' following a 3-0 defeat at Oldham the previous evening. An extremely unpopular appointment in the first place, Megson did nothing by results to endear himself to the Forest faithful, being unable to prevent the club from sliding into the third tier for the first time since 1951. He left the club just four points above the League One relegation zone.

SATURDAY 17th FEBRUARY 1962

David Pleat made his debut for Forest in a home game against Cardiff City and, at 17 years and 33 days, became the youngest player ever to appear in a league game for the club. It was a goalscoring debut as well, earning his club a 2-1 win after Johnny Quigley had scored the first. Pleat would only play six games for the Reds, but years later he became a successful football manager at Luton Town.

FRIDAY 17th FEBRUARY 2006

Forest announced the appointment of reserve team boss Ian McParland and assistant manager Frank Barlow as joint caretaker managers following the end of Gary Megson's managerial stint for the Reds. The Barlow-McParland combination would work wonders, driving Forest up the table and into genuine contention for the play-offs, although they would ultimately fall just short. Barlow left the club at the end of the season, and McParland stayed on the staff until he left for Notts County in October 2007.

FRIDAY 18th FEBRUARY 1944

Henry Newton was born in Nottingham. Initially a left-back, Newton would move into the half-back line with great success and become one of the finest left-halves in the country. He won four England U23 caps but never managed to break into the national side despite being named in a number of squads. A member of the great 1966/67 side, Newton fell victim of Matt Gillies' cull of that team and joined Everton in 1970 for £115,000, moving on to Derby County in 1973 where he won a championship medal in 1974/75.

WEDNESDAY 19th FEBRUARY 1975

Brian Clough made an expected double-signing in rescuing John McGovern and John O'Hare from their Leeds United nightmares and bringing them back under his wing at the City Ground. McGovern had been with Clough at Hartlepool United and Derby County before following him to Elland Road. O'Hare arrived at the Baseball Ground from Sunderland for £20,000 in 1967. Both players had been frozen out at Elland Rad since the end of Clough's brief reign at the club, so they probably welcomed the chance to get involved on matchdays again, and both would go on to make contributions to Forest's glory years.

MONDAY 19th FEBRUARY 1996

The weather was the only winner as Forest's televised fifth round cup tie at the City Ground against Tottenham Hotspur was abandoned after 15 minutes when a blizzard descended upon Nottingham. The tie would be played more than a week later, ending in a 2-2 draw. Forest won the replay at White Hart Lane on penalties.

SATURDAY 20th FEBRUARY 1971

Journeyman forward Neil Martin made his debut for Forest at home to Burnley following his transfer from Coventry City. Martin had already scored more than 100 goals in Scottish football with Alloa, Queen of the South and Hibernian before moving to the English game in 1965 with Sunderland. Martin completed a second century of goals at Forest, moving on to Brighton & Hove Albion in 1975 and Crystal Palace in 1976.

SATURDAY 21st FEBRUARY 1976

Right-back Liam O'Kane was taken off after 24 minutes in a game at Bristol City with a serious leg injury. A regular Northern Ireland international, O'Kane had been with the club since signing from Derry City in December 1968. Initially a centre-back, Liam moved to right-back in place of Peter Hindley in the early 1970s, and recovered from a broken leg suffered in 1971. This time, however, there was to be no way back and O'Kane's career was over at the age of 28. Brian Clough would offer O'Kane a coaching role at the club, a position the Irishman would retain until leaving in 2005 after 36 years of service.

SATURDAY 21st FEBRUARY 1981

Martin O'Neill's long career at Nottingham Forest came to a close with a home game against Arsenal. Signed from the Irish League side Distillery in 1971 from under the noses of a number of clubs, O'Neill was another player – like John Robertson – with unfulfilled potential who seemed on his way out of Forest until Brian Clough arrived at the City Ground. O'Neill would then go on to become one of the best midfielders in the country, usually (and begrudgingly, as O'Neill always saw himself as a central midfielder) on the right of midfield. He was an automatic selection for and eventually captain of Northern Ireland, and his tally of 36 caps during his time at the club remained a record until Stuart Pearce surpassed it. O'Neill scored twice in his final game to secure a 3-1 win before moving to Norwich City. The switch was supposedly an exchange deal for Justin Fashanu, although that side of the deal fell through (Fashanu would join the club in the summer). The Irishman would of course go on to be a highly successful football manager with Leicester City, Celtic and Aston Villa.

TUESDAY 22nd FEBRUARY 1978

Forest were on their way to Wembley for the first time since 1959! A firm 4-2 win over Leeds United (goals by Withe, Bowyer, O'Neill and Woodcock) added to the 3-1 first leg victory at Elland Road to give Forest a 7-3 aggregate win and a place in the League Cup final against Liverpool, who edged out Arsenal 2-1 on aggregate in the other semi-final.

SATURDAY 22nd FEBRUARY 2003

The days when the fledgling Marlon Harewood couldn't find the net even when armed with a map and compass were completely erased when the now-lethal frontman scored four goals before half-time in a game at home to basement-dwelling Stoke City. He completed his hat-trick before the half-hour and made it four from the spot on the stroke of half-time when Petur Marteinsson handballed in the box. He would have been the first player to score five in a game since 'Sandy' Higgins in January 1891 if he had notched another. Forest won 6-0 in the end, the other two goals coming from David Johnson and Eoin Jess.

MONDAY 23rd FEBRUARY 1959

Forest moved into the quarter-finals of the FA Cup with a handsome 5-0 victory over Birmingham City at Filbert Street in a second replay of the original fifth round tie after two 1-1 draws. Right-winger Roy Dwight netted a hat-trick, with a Billy Gray brace – one a penalty – completing the scoring.

SATURDAY 24th FEBRUARY 1979

Finally, the first sighting of record signing Trevor Francis in a Forest shirt in a league game, after matches for Forest's 'A' team and in testimonials against Exeter City and West Bromwich Albion. The million pound man came on as a second-half substitute for Martin O'Neill. Forest won the game 2-1 thanks to early goals from David Needham and Garry Birtles.

MONDAY 24th FEBRUARY 1997

The financial future of Nottingham Forest (reportedly £8 million in debt) was finally settled when shareholders voted by 189 to 7 to accept a bid of £16 million from the Bridgford plc consortium of local author Phil Soar, Saracens owner Nigel Wray and former Tottenham Hotspur chairman Irving Scholar.

WEDNESDAY 25th FEBRUARY 1976

Forest pair Bert Bowery and Tony Woodcock made their debuts and both scored in a 6-0 win over Southport. The only downside to this was that they were on loan to Lincoln City at the time.

SATURDAY 25th FEBRUARY 1978

A thrilling game at Norwich City in which Forest raced into a three goal lead within 25 minutes thanks to goals from Peter Withe, Colin Barrett and Martin O'Neill. However, in an uncharacteristic defensive capitulation, the hosts were allowed back into the game, John Ryan converting a penalty just before half-time, followed by two goals in three minutes from Colin Suggett and Keith Robson to rescue a 3-3 draw.

SUNDAY 25th FEBRUARY 1990

The Reds were off to Wembley yet again, grinding out a 0-0 draw at Coventry City. They won this Littlewoods Cup semi-final tie thanks to a 2-1 win at the City Ground in the first leg.

SATURDAY 25th FEBRUARY 2006

The dark and dismal days of Gary Megson's reign seemed a million years ago as Forest welcomed Swindon Town to the City Ground and hammered them 7-1. The Barlow/McParland-inspired Reds were all over Swindon from the off, right-midfielder Nicky Southall scoring after three minutes, then completing the only hat-trick of his career with goals in the 51st and 55th minutes. Wes Morgan popped up with two and his defensive partner Ian Breckin also scored. Swindon had Jerel Ifil sent off after 66 minutes for his second booking but Forest were already 6-0 up by then. Trevor Benjamin netted a consolation before sub Jack Lester completed the rout.

SATURDAY 26th FEBRUARY 1966

Forest announced the capture of England international Joe Baker from Arsenal for £65,000. The first player ever to play for England without having played in English football (he was born in Liverpool but moved to Motherwell at a young age after beginning his career at Hibs), Joe had been a prolific scorer at Arsenal but was surprisingly allowed to leave after a poor 1965/66 season. The Gunners' loss was Forest's gain and the Trent Enders soon had a new hero, with cries of 'zigga zagga' echoing around the City Ground whenever the speedy centre forward embarked on one of his pacy runs. Baker was sold to Sunderland in 1969 for £30,000, and sadly passed away in October 2003, aged a mere 63.

MONDAY 26th FEBRUARY 1979

Forest were knocked out of the FA Cup at the fifth round stage by Arsenal thanks to Frank Stapleton's conversion of a Liam Brady cross. The Reds' supporters trudged home with an unfamiliar feeling – defeat! This was the first time Forest had lost at the City Ground since April 23rd 1977, when a Peter Sayer goal gave Cardiff City a 1-0 victory.

SUNDAY 26th FEBRUARY 1989

It had been a while, and it was a lot tougher than it should have been, but Nottingham Forest would play a cup final at Wembley for the first time since the unexpected 1-0 loss to Wolverhampton Wanderers in the 1981 League Cup final. Forest booked their trip down to the capital by the skin of their teeth with a 1-0 second leg win over third tier Bristol City at a rain-drenched Ashton Gate in the Littlewoods Cup. The first leg had been a dour affair, with Paul Mardon's opener having been cancelled out by an unlucky own-goal by John Pender, but the second leg was a corker, with City totally matching the then fourth best-placed team in the country. With seconds to go City's Alan Walsh turned, shot but hit the post; the ball got trapped between Forest's Steve Sutton's legs and somehow stayed out. In extra time City finally made a mistake, leaving Garry Parker free to crash a shot past Keith Waugh. Luton Town now awaited at Wembley, having disposed of West Ham United in the other semi-final.

THURSDAY 27th FEBRUARY 1997

In a surprise appointment, ex-Wimbledon and Sheffield United boss Dave Bassett left his role as manager of Crystal Palace and became the general manager at Forest. Brought in by the new board with alleged promises of a 'job for life' to help fledging caretaker boss Stuart Pearce, it was reported that 'Psycho' was not exactly favourable concerning his new co-manager. The pair failed to save Forest from relegation, and when Pearce left for Newcastle United at the end of the season, Bassett took on full managerial duties. This turned out to be a successful move, as Bassett took Forest back to the top flight at the first attempt, thanks mainly to the lethal strike-force of Pierre van Hooijdonk and Kevin Campbell. Bassett's time with the Reds lasted until January 1999 when a rock-bottom Forest relieved him of his duties.

SATURDAY 28th FEBRUARY 1948

One of the heroes of Forest's 1950/51 promotion campaign, Horace Gager, made his debut against Leicester at the City Ground, following his transfer from Luton Town. Born in London in 1917, Gager was playing for Vauxhall Motors before signing up for the Hatters, making three appearances before the outbreak of World War II. By the time football returned, Gager was in his thirties, having missed out on the best years of his career. He was a commanding centre-half and was made club captain in succession to Bob McCall in 1951. Having led the club to promotion Gager played until his late thirties, retiring in 1955. He passed away in 1984.

SATURDAY 28th FEBRUARY 1970

Forest's terrible luck with goalkeepers continued when custodian Alan Hill broke his arm in a 1-1 draw with Everton at the City Ground. Hill had been signed from Rotherham United in 1969 as cover for Peter Grummitt, having joined the Millers from his hometown club of Barnsley in 1966. The virtually unknown Hill had impressed so much between the sticks that the long-serving Grummitt was allowed to leave for Sheffield Wednesday. Hill's broken arm turned out to be so serious he was advised never to play again, retiring at the age of 28. Robbed of Hill, Forest took Mansfield Town's ex-Newcastle United keeper Dave Hollins on loan for the rest of the season in exchange for Duncan McKenzie. Hill would return to the City Ground on various occasions and in various capacities in the 1980s and 1990s.

MONDAY 29th FEBRUARY 1904

The prize for the only known Forest player to be born on the 29th of February goes to Ralph John Langtrey Lynas, a Belfast-born inside-left who made 20 appearances for the club between 1925 and 1926. Ralph won Irish League and Irish Amateur caps and, as well as Forest, turned out for Cliftonville and Ards.

FRIDAY 29th FEBRUARY 1980

Brian Clough failed to be lured into European football, turning down a job offer from the Greek side Olympiacos CF Piraeus.

NOTTINGHAM FOREST
On This Day

MARCH

SATURDAY 1st MARCH 1930

A record City Ground crowd of 44,166 paid 1s 9d to watch then-Second Division Forest take on the First Division leaders, Sheffield Wednesday, in the sixth round of the FA Cup. Wednesday were 2-0 up within 17 minutes, but the Reds upped the fight and three minutes before half-time a Bob Morton pass was seized upon by Joe Loftus, who rounded two defenders before shooting home from inside the area. With the crowd urging the underdogs on, Forest pulled level just before the hour mark when Billy Dickinson received the ball from Bob Wallace and fired the ball in off the post from 13 yards. It finished 2-2, then, but Forest went down 3-1 at Hillsborough in the replay.

SUNDAY 1st MARCH 1992

The Reds were on their way to Wembley again! In a second leg tie at White Hart Lane in the Rumbelows Cup, Forest ran out 2-1 winners, going through on aggregate after drawing the first leg 1-1 at the City Ground. The match was held up for over an hour thanks to a false terrorist bomb threat, but when play did get underway Forest were ahead after ten minutes, Scot Gemmill and Lee Glover cleverly working an opening which saw the latter convert. Spurs were level five minutes later when Gary Lineker headed home from Gordon Durie's precise lob. In extra time Forest found the winner, Roy Keane rising above everyone to glance home Gary Crosby's corner.

SATURDAY 2nd MARCH 1996

A routine 3-1 win over Sheffield Wednesday at Hillsborough, made significant by Wednesday playing the entire second half with Steve Nicol in goal after ex-Red Chris Woods had gone off injured at half-time. Nicol conceded two of the goals – one a minute after the restart from Paul McGregor, the other a glancing header from Bryan Roy.

SUNDAY 3rd MARCH 1974

Forest continued with their Sunday football experiment and welcomed Notts County from across the Trent for the first league game ever played at the City Ground on a Sunday. A bumper crowd of 29,962 – easily the highest of the season – turned out, but were unrewarded by a fairly tame goalless draw.

SATURDAY 3rd MARCH 1990

One of the oddest and most infamous goals in footballing history. Seven minutes into the second half of a game at the City Ground against Manchester City a Garry Parker cross was taken cleanly by City keeper Andy Dibble. As Dibble waited for his defence to clear the box he took one hand off the ball, unaware that Forest right-winger Gary Crosby was behind him. Crosby cleanly headed the ball off Dibble's palm and side-footed it into the net. To the amazement of Dibble and his team-mates, referee Roger Gifford gave the goal. Howard Kendall's men spent the remainder of the game kicking Forest players into the air, but Forest won 1-0.

WEDNESDAY 4th MARCH 1931

In a rare example of 1930s European football, Forest travelled to Rotterdam to take on a Netherlands XI, winning 3-1 with goals from Johnny Dent (penalty), Billy Dickinson and Harry Smith.

WEDNESDAY 5th MARCH 1958

The Reds announced the long-awaited capture of lethal Northern Irish marksman Francis 'Fay' Coyle. A prolific striker, Coyle had once scored 13 goals in the Irish League in a single week. Alas, the move fell flat and a homesick Coyle only played three times for Forest before returning to Ireland after the 1958 World Cup.

SATURDAY 5th MARCH 1994

A debut against Luton Town at the City Ground for striker Jason Lee. Lee would become infamous for his tied-up dreadlocks hairstyle, for which the Forest fans would sing 'he's got a pineapple, on his head' in time to the 1978 record 'We've Got The Whole World in Our Hands'. This was initially in appreciation of Lee's whole-hearted application (if not ability), but later became adopted as a taunt by opposition supporters following Frank Skinner and David Baddiel's unnecessary belittling of the striker on their *Fantasy Football* television show. Lee's form would suffer as a result, although he recovered enough to finish as the club's joint-leading league goalscorer in 1995/96 with eight goals from 21 starts. Lee left Forest in 1997 and embarked on a nomadic career which saw him still playing local non-league football at the age of 39.

FRIDAY 5th MARCH 1999

Ron Atkinson's 'all hands to the pumps' approach to save Forest from relegation continued with the acquisition of 36-year-old Richard Gough on loan from San Jose Clash. Unlike fellow new boys John Harkes, Carlton Palmer and Stale Stensaas, Gough was a massive hit with the Forest faithful, who demanded his permanent capture. However, Gough's re-emergence into British football alerted his former Rangers boss, Walter Smith, at Everton, and Gough ended up playing in the centre of the Toffeemen's defence for a further two seasons.

SATURDAY 6th MARCH 2011

George Boyd made his debut on loan from Peterborough United against Swansea City at the City Ground. Dubbed 'The White Pele' by his adoring Posh fans, Boyd was expected to sign permanently at the end of the season, but his lack of fitness failed to impress Forest boss Billy Davies, so Boyd returned to London Road where he signed a new contract for the Posh.

SATURDAY 7th MARCH 1959

Manager Billy Walker rested regulars 'Chic' Thomson, Bob McKinlay, Jack Burkitt and Johnny Quigley and paid for it, losing 7-1 at home to Birmingham City. Winger Roy Dwight scored Forest's only goal, and it was a personal disaster for ex-Sunderland custodian Willie Fraser, who let in seven on his Forest debut.

SATURDAY 7th MARCH 2001

An ankle injury obtained in a home game against Barnsley ended the temporary Forest career of popular right-sided American Ben Olsen. Olsen had been signed on loan by David Platt from his MLS club DC United in October and impressed sufficiently to suggest a permanent deal to bring him to English football at the City Ground was on the cards. The ankle injury put paid to any chance of that and he returned to the US. It would take a full year, but happily the energetic Olsen would make a complete recovery. Back at DC United, Olsen would make one appearance for the USA in the 2006 World Cup finals, and go on to captain and then manage his only American club.

SATURDAY 8th MARCH 1986

A final appearance in a Forest shirt for Old Trafford-bound Peter Davenport at Portman Road in a 1-0 defeat to Ipswich Town. Four days later he headed to Manchester United for £750,000. Davenport would start well at United, scoring 16 goals in all competitions in 1987/88, but Alex Ferguson's re-signing of Mark Hughes in 1988 would mark the end for the Birkenhead-born marksman, who joined Middlesbrough.

WEDNESDAY 8th MARCH 2000

Forest's recent signing, Jack Lester, opened his account for his new side with one of the quickest goals in Forest's history – after a mere 14 seconds. From kick-off the ball was rolled back to Ricky Scimeca, whose lob into the Norwich City box was missed by Matt Jackson. The ball fell nicely to Dougie Freedman, who flicked it across to Lester to net past Andy Marshall from 15 yards.

SATURDAY 9th MARCH 1974

A day that should have been glorious for Forest instead ended up as farce, as an in-form Reds side took on out-of-form Newcastle United at St James' Park in an FA Cup quarter-final tie. Ian Bowyer had Forest ahead in less than two minutes and at half-time it was 2-1 to the visitors, Forest's second from Liam O'Kane. Almost on the hour things got even better when Forest were awarded a penalty (converted by George Lyall) and Pat Howard was sent off for pushing the referee. Two goals ahead and with an extra player, what could go wrong? How about several hundred United fans invading the pitch from the Leazes End? The referee took the players off for ten minutes while order was restored (but not soon enough for centre-half Dave Serella, who was punched), but once the game was back on Forest's concentration was gone and goals by Terry McDermott, John Tudor and Bobby Moncur saw the Magpies win 4-3. Forest lodged an appeal, the FA declared the match void and a replay was ordered at Goodison Park, ending 0-0. Having drawn the first tie Forest reasonably expected a replay at the City Ground, but the FA ordered another game at Goodison Park. Malcolm Macdonald scored the only goal of that game and Forest were out, having played a cup tie over three games, yet, through no fault of their own, none of them at home.

SUNDAY 9th MARCH 1997

The new owners of Nottingham Forest, Bridgford plc, announced the capture of Celtic striker Pierre van Hooijdonk. Bought too late to save the club from relegation that season, van Hooijdonk would go on to score a ridiculous amount of goals the following term.

WEDNESDAY 10th MARCH 1920

An awful afternoon for Forest as they lost 8-0 in a Division Two match against Birmingham City. Down to ten men in the first half through Horace Hart's broken collarbone, the Reds couldn't contain Birmingham's forwards – especially Harry Hampton, who scored four.

TUESDAY 10th MARCH 1964

A record day for the Reds as they broke their transfer record by paying £40,000 for Arsenal wing-half John Barnwell. The Geordie would become a regular in the Forest side for six years before joining Sheffield United in 1970. Moving into management, Barnwell would lead his Wolverhampton Wanderers side to victory over Forest in the 1980 League Cup final, and he became chief executive of the League Managers' Association in July 1996.

SATURDAY 11th MARCH 1978

An all-conquering Forest side proved they were occasionally human after all, losing 2-0 to West Bromwich Albion at the Hawthorns in an FA Cup quarter-final to end dreams of the league, League Cup and FA Cup treble. Mick Martin and Cyrille Regis scored the goals which sent the Reds crashing.

SUNDAY 12th MARCH 1905

The birth of Tommy Graham, one of Forest's heroes of the 1920s and 1930s, in Consett, County Durham. A superb and underrated stopper, Graham was picked up by Forest in July 1927 from Consett Celtic and soon became a regular in the heart of the club's defence. It was tragic that he only won two caps for England, but his loyalty to Second Division Forest for a decade put paid to a regular spot with the national side. Tommy would remain with Forest once he had retired in 1939, and 20 years later he was Forest's trainer in the 1959 FA Cup final win.

SULKY STRIKER PIERRE VAN HOOIJDONK, FAMED FOR HIS ONE-MAN STRIKE IN 1999, JOINED FOREST FROM CELTIC ON 9TH MARCH 1997

SATURDAY 12th MARCH 1977

A surprise signing from Long Eaton United, Garry Birtles, made his debut against Hull City on the right wing. It would take 18 months for Birtles to make a second appearance.

SATURDAY 12th MARCH 1988

Brian Clough took one step closer to that elusive first FA Cup final appearance as Forest unexpectedly beat Arsenal at Highbury in a quarter-final tie. It was two of the lesser lights of the Forest side who sent the Reds through – Paul Wilkinson volleyed home from just outside the area shortly before half-time, and Brian Rice ran onto Nigel Clough's exquisite lofted pass to chip John Lukic. David Rocastle pulled one back with a minute to go.

SATURDAY 13th MARCH 1909

Forest's FA Cup progress came to a shuddering halt in the fourth round against Derby County at the Baseball Ground. The Reds lost 3-0, thanks mainly to an Alf Bentley hat-trick, and had Enoch 'Knocker' West sent off to add to their troubles.

SATURDAY 13th MARCH 1976

Possibly the most unsung member of Forest's 1977/78 championship-winning side, Colin Barrett, made his debut on loan from Manchester City at home to Fulham. Barrett's finest moment came in the first leg of the first round of the 1978/79 European Cup against Liverpool, scoring the crucial second goal with a rather special volley.

TUESDAY 14th MARCH 1939

The former England international and Aston Villa legend Billy Walker was appointed manager of Nottingham Forest, succeeding Harry Wightman. A tremendously popular man, Walker would go on to manage the club for more than 21 years and, despite seeing them relegated to the Third Division South in 1949, would guide the club all the way back up the league ladder to the top flight in 1957 and to FA Cup final glory in 1959. He retired due to ailing health in 1960, and Forest and Villa fans were united in grief upon Walker's death in 1964.

SATURDAY 14th MARCH 1959

Forest were on their way to Wembley for the first time in their history, reaching the FA Cup final for the first time since 1898. Despite being the slight underdogs in their semi-final tie at Hillsborough against Aston Villa, Billy Walker saw his red-shirted heroes triumph over the club he served for more than 15 years. Inside-forward Johnny Quigley scored the only goal of a tight game. Awaiting Forest at Wembley were Luton Town, who despatched plucky Third Division side Norwich City out of the competition after a replay.

SATURDAY 15th MARCH 1902

FA Cup semi-final day in England, and Forest travelled to White Hart Lane to take on Southampton of the Southern League. A smallpox epidemic meant that only 200 or so supporters travelled down to see the Reds lose 3-1, Forest's goal coming from Jack Calvey. Southampton would go on to lose the final at Crystal Palace to Sheffield United.

SATURDAY 15th MARCH 1980

Hot favourites to complete a hat-trick of League Cup wins, it was an enormous shock when Forest lost 1-0 to Wolverhampton Wanderers at Wembley. On 67 minutes, a long punt up the field by Peter Daniel was chested down by Forest defender David Needham, who then collided with Peter Shilton, the ball rolling nicely into the path of Andy Gray to score an open goal from six yards out. Ex-Liverpool and England defender Emlyn Hughes collected the trophy that had been held by Forest since 1978. Forest: Shilton, Anderson, Gray, McGovern, Needham, Burns, O'Neill, Bowyer, Birtles, Francis, Robertson.

FRIDAY 16th MARCH 1956

Veteran striker Doug Lishman was signed from Arsenal in an attempt to bolster Forest's forward line. Hardly a spring chicken at 32, the signing was a good 'un as Lishman scored six goals in 11 games at the end of the 1955/56 season, then 13 in 22 in the first half of the next, before an injury ruled him out until March. Lishman managed six more games and three more goals before retiring that summer.

FRIDAY 16th MARCH 1979

Preston North End paid a record fee of £95,000 for young Forest striker Steve Elliott. Elliott would never quite fulfil his potential, although he would go on to be a regular scorer in the lower divisions. A second bite at the top-flight cherry in 1984/85 with Luton Town would fail to pay dividends.

SATURDAY 17th MARCH 1979

Forest became the first club to retain the League Cup when they beat Southampton 3-2 at Wembley. The Saints took an unexpected lead through a neatly-worked David Peach goal on 16 minutes, and went into the break a goal to the good. Forest took charge in the second half and the magnificent forward pairing of Tony Woodcock and Garry Birtles tore the Southampton defence to shreds. Birtles scored twice (51 and 79) and had another two disallowed, with Woodcock weighing in after 83 minutes. Nick Holmes edged his side back into it with two minutes to go but Forest held firm. Forest: Shilton, Barrett, Clark, McGovern, Lloyd, Needham, O'Neill, Gemmill, Birtles, Woodcock, Robertson.

SATURDAY 17th MARCH 2007

Double debut day for Forest as youngster Brendan Moloney and the slightly more experienced Alan Wright, signed on loan from Sheffield United, made their first appearances for the club in a 1-0 home win over Gillingham.

SATURDAY 18th MARCH 1978

Forest's first taste of Wembley action for almost 20 years in the League Cup final against Liverpool. Forest were second favourites for this game, missing Peter Shilton, Archie Gemmill, David Needham (all cup-tied) and Colin Barrett (injured). Forest had no back-up in goal aside from an 18-year-old Chris Woods. Woods would turn out to be the hero of the day, as Forest's outfield largely froze, leaving Liverpool free to batter the defence and Woods' goal. The youngster pulled several saves out of the top drawer to secure a 0-0 draw and earn a replay four days later. Forest: Woods, Anderson, Clark, McGovern (O'Hare), Lloyd, Burns, O'Neill, Bowyer, Withe, Woodcock, Robertson.

SATURDAY 18th MARCH 1989

Further cup joy for Forest's best team since the late 1970s when they beat Manchester United 1-0 at Old Trafford in an FA Cup quarter-final thanks to a Garry Parker finish from a Franz Carr cross. This meant Forest's second successive FA Cup semi-final, again drawing Liverpool.

WEDNESDAY 19th MARCH 1980

A glorious evening for Forest, turning around a 1-0 home deficit from the first leg of the European Cup quarter-final against Dinamo Berlin to win 3-2 on aggregate in East Germany. The £1 million man, Trevor Francis, was key to the victory, as his two goals put the Reds ahead on aggregate. A John Robertson penalty put Forest 3-0 up before half-time, then Frank Terletzki scored from the spot for Dinamo after 49 minutes to give the East Germans forlorn hope. It wasn't to be, and Forest marched on towards a final in Madrid.

SUNDAY 19th MARCH 1978

League leaders for much of the season, Forest suddenly found themselves in the disappointing position of 24th. Thankfully this was in the UK Top 40, and 'We've Got The Whole World in Our Hands' by Nottingham Forest FC with Paper Lace slammed into the charts a mere four places outside the top 20.

TUESDAY 19th MARCH 1996

The Reds went into a UEFA quarter-final tie at home to Bayern Munich with high hopes, having only lost the first leg in Germany 2-1, their goal coming from the head of Steve Chettle. Sadly it was not to be, as England's only remaining representatives in European football were beaten 5-1 and 7-2 on aggregate.

SATURDAY 20th MARCH 1971

A double milestone for Forest in a 3-2 victory over Everton. Peter Cormack scored twice, recording the 4,000th league goal of Forest's history. Forest's other goal came from Ian Storey-Moore – his 100th for the club.

MONDAY 20th MARCH 1978

The Professional Footballers' Association announced a double victory for Nottingham Forest, with goalkeeper Peter Shilton netting the Player of the Season award and striker Tony Woodcock earning the Young Player of the Season award. Ridiculously, only Shilton and John Robertson made it into 'Team of the Year'. The absence of future Sportswriters' Player of the Season Kenny Burns was also rather puzzling.

SATURDAY 21st MARCH 1896

A debut for full-back Jimmy Iremonger in an away game at Stoke. As well as playing more than 300 games for Forest and winning three England caps, Jimmy was also known as a first-class cricketer with more than 300 appearances for Notts. His brother, Albert, played almost 600 games for Notts County in goal and also played cricket for Notts.

TUESDAY 21st MARCH 1972

A personal triumph for Forest's young striker Duncan McKenzie, who defeated full-back Peter Hindley in the club's inaugural annual players' darts tournament. McKenzie would reach the final the following year, but this time would only see what he could have won as he lost to midfielder Barry Lyons.

THURSDAY 22nd MARCH 1866

The first recorded game for the 'Forest Football Club' took place on the Forest Recreation Ground, their opponents being the 'Notts Football Club'. The pair, of course, would eventually evolve into Nottingham Forest and Notts County. Despite having 17 players as opposed to Notts' 11, Forest could not make such an advantage tell, and the game ended 0-0.

SATURDAY 22nd MARCH 1975

A rarity here, as Nottingham Forest took on Manchester United in a Second Division game, the temporarily-fallen giants having been relegated from the top flight the previous term. United took the spoils at the City Ground with a 1-0 victory via a Gerry Daly goal.

WEDNESDAY 22nd MARCH 1978

Forest got their hands on their first proper piece of silverware under the stewardship of Brian Clough. Following a 0-0 draw the previous Saturday, this replayed League Cup final at Old Trafford went Forest's way thanks to a dubious decision by referee Pat Partridge. Nearly ten minutes into the second half John O'Hare was through on goal when he was tripped by defender Phil Thompson. Despite the challenge being inches outside the area the ref gave a penalty which John Robertson naturally converted. Partridge also disallowed a Liverpool goal, and afterwards Liverpool's Tommy Smith suggested the referee 'should be shot'. No matter, it was captain-for-the-evening Kenny Burns who hoisted the trophy aloft to the delight of Forest fans who had journeyed to Manchester. Forest: Woods; Anderson, Clark, O'Hare, Lloyd, Burns, O'Neill, Bowyer, Withe, Woodcock, Robertson.

SATURDAY 23rd MARCH 1889

Forest's first-ever floodlit game took place on this day, a friendly at home to local rivals Notts Rangers under 'Welles Lights', which had a luminescence of 4,000 candles. The artificial illumination did nothing for Forest, who went down 2-0.

SATURDAY 23rd MARCH 1935

Johnny Dent scored a hat-trick for the second game in succession at the City Ground game against Burnley, following his three goals at Boundary Park the previous week against Oldham Athletic. With pleasing symmetry, both games finished 5-0 to Forest and the other scorer in both games was Tom Peacock with a brace. Dent, who managed 13 goals in only 18 games in an injury-hit season, had been signed from Huddersfield Town in 1930 and scored 122 goals in 206 games before leaving for Kidderminster in 1937. Johnny passed away in 1979.

SATURDAY 24th MARCH 1883

A day of bad travel for Forest as they arrived two hours late for a friendly at Darwen. The paying spectators had their money refunded and the game was completed in near darkness, Forest losing 4-2.

MONDAY 24th MARCH 1947

Archibald 'Archie' Gemmill was born in Paisley, Renfrewshire. A key member of the championship-winning side, Gemmill was signed from Brian Clough's former team Derby County in October 1977 for £25,000 and John Middleton, having been signed by Clough for Derby from Preston in September 1970. Gemmill was an industrious playmaker, speedy and with bags of skill, as emphasised by his famous goal against Holland for Scotland in the 1978 World Cup finals in which he beat three players before slipping the ball neatly past Jan Jongbloed. Gemmill allegedly fell out with Clough over his omission from the 1979 European Cup final team despite declaring himself fit. He left Forest far too soon in 1979, going on to play for Birmingham City, Wigan Athletic and Derby County again. It took Clough four years to replace him. Gemmill would return to coach at Forest in 1984 after he had retired from playing.

SATURDAY 25th MARCH 1961

Jack Burkitt made his 500th appearance for Forest in a 1-1 home draw with Wolverhampton Wanderers. A stalwart in Forest's rearguard since signing from Darlaston in 1947, Jack was a model professional, firm but fair and a true gentleman of the game. He captained Forest to their FA Cup win in 1959 and ended up lifting the famous trophy as Forest beat Luton. After the game Jack only played three more times for the club before retiring, his appearances representing a record later surpassed by his defensive colleague Bobby McKinlay. He joined the coaching staff before leaving in 1966 to manage Notts County for a year, and then joined the Derby County coaching staff under a certain Brian Clough. Ill health forced him out of football in 1969, and Jack passed away in 2003.

TUESDAY 25th MARCH 1975

Notts County became the first team to play 3,000 league matches and, fittingly, Forest were their Meadow Lane opponents. In a thrilling contest, Ian Scanlon put the Magpies ahead, with George Lyall equalising for Forest five minutes before the break. County took a 2-1 lead when Paul Richardson hit a backpass into his own net just before the hour, but his embarrassment was tempered when Barry Butlin headed in a cross after 77 minutes to complete the 2-2 draw.

SATURDAY 26th MARCH 1983

A defeat at Southampton saw Forest complete a miserable run of ten games without a win, easily the worst spell since the first two months of Brian Clough's reign as manager. The curse was broken a week later with a 2-0 home win over Everton, Forest going on to storm the rest of the 1982/83 season, winning seven and drawing two of their last nine league games.

SATURDAY 27th MARCH 1880

Forest played in the semi-finals of the FA Cup for the first time today, defeating Notts County, Turton, Blackburn Rovers and Sheffield en route. Despite being favourites for the game, the Reds lost 1-0 to Oxford University at the Kennington Oval. The university XI would go on to lose 1-0 to Clapham Rovers in the final, at the same venue.

MONDAY 27th MARCH 1961

The City Ground hosted an FA Cup semi-final tie, the first in Nottingham since 1925 (Cardiff City beating Blackburn Rovers 3-1 at Meadow Lane), with Leicester City taking on Sheffield United in a replay after a 0-0 draw at Elland Road.

TUESDAY 28th MARCH 1910

Percy Ashton was born in West Melton. Ashton joined Forest in 1930 from Melton Excelsior, but had to wait a few years before he displaced Alf Dexter in the Forest goal. Ashton continued to battle Dexter for the green woollen jersey throughout his career, with both keepers prone to the odd mistake. Ashton's career ended at the beginning of World War II.

WEDNESDAY 28th MARCH 1979

Danny Blanchflower's bottom-placed Chelsea came to the City Ground and were soundly beaten 6-0, mainly thanks to an inspired display as an attacking midfielder by expensive signing Trevor Francis. Francis failed to score himself, but had a hand in most of the other strikes, including Martin O'Neill's only hat-trick for Forest. The other scorers were Tony Woodcock (with a brace) and Garry Birtles.

MONDAY 29th MARCH 1948

An Easter Monday game at home to Southampton which finished 1-1 marked the final appearance for the Reds by winger Tom Johnston. Robbed of the early years of his career by World War II, Johnston signed for Forest in 1944 and became arguably Forest's best player once football had recommenced. He made the trip across the river in 1948 to sign for County and served the Magpies excellently for eight years, supplying many of the crosses for Tommy Lawton.

SATURDAY 30th MARCH 1968

Promising keeper Mick Harby made his debut for Forest at home to Sunderland, the Reds losing 3-0. Harby's next two games were even worse, losing 6-1 to Wolverhampton Wanderers at Molineux and then to Liverpool by the same score. He never got to correct his unwanted distinction of conceding 15 goals in the only three games of his Forest career.

SATURDAY 30th MARCH 1991

Winger Tony Loughlan made a telling first-ever touch in professional football, as he converted for Forest after only 36 seconds against Wimbledon at Plough Lane, although Forest would go on to lose the game 3-1. Loughlan would only play one more game for Forest before he was released in 1993.

WEDNESDAY 31st MARCH 1982

Out-of-favour midfielder Gary Mills moved to Seattle Sounders on a temporary year-long contract. Seattle would loan Mills briefly to Derby County in 1983, where he would appear against Forest in an FA Cup third round tie. Mills found his way back to Forest and remained there until 1987, when he joined local rivals Notts County along with Garry Birtles.

MONDAY 31st MARCH 1986

Forest centre-back Mark Smalley made an appearance whilst on loan at Birmingham City…against Nottingham Forest. Despite the young defender's presence, the Blues went down 3-0.

NOTTINGHAM FOREST
On This Day

APRIL

TUESDAY 1st APRIL 1975

The fools today were Sheffield Wednesday, who were relegated to the third tier for the first time in their history after Forest beat them 1-0 through a George Lyall penalty following Danny Cameron's foul in the box on Barry Butlin. It was only Forest's second league win since Brian Clough took over, the first being his first league game in charge nearly three months beforehand.

SATURDAY 1st APRIL 1995

More All Fool's Day misery for Sheffield Wednesday, as in a Premiership clash they were beaten 7-1 at Hillsborough by Forest. The tormentor-in-chief was Stan Collymore, who mesmerised the Wednesday defence with his pace and power, getting two of the goals. The others came from Stuart Pearce, Ian Woan, Bryan Roy (2) and Lars Bohinen, with a Mark Bright penalty the only blemish on Mark Crossley's quiet afternoon. Forest's record for the highest away victory in the Premiership stood for two years until Manchester United's 8-1 mauling of a certain Nottingham Forest.

FRIDAY 2nd APRIL 1976

Edward 'Teddy' Paul Sheringham was born in Highams Park, London. One of Forest's most expensive signings, Sheringham was bought by Brian Clough in July 1991 for £2 million, galvanising Forest's attack until his unexpected sale 13 months later to Tottenham Hotspur. Sheringham's career blossomed and he became one of English football's most potent forwards for both club and country, winning a Champions League winners' medal with Manchester United in 1999.

WEDNESDAY 2nd APRIL 1986

The City Ground witnessed one of the fiercest shots in football history from a free kick via the right boot of Johnny Metgod in a league match against West Ham. From well outside the penalty area, and with a run-up that started within touching distance of the halfway line, Metgod hit an unstoppable shot of such ferocity that if it hadn't been caught by Phil Parkes' net it would have continued onwards into orbit around the Earth.

SUNDAY 3rd APRIL 1910

Danny Edgar was born in Jarrow. He would become Forest's regular right-back upon signing from Sunderland in 1935 until his retirement in 1938 due to a cartilage injury. He began his career with his local side, St Bede's, before joining Walsall in August 1930 and then becoming a Rokerite a year later. Danny passed away in 1991.

SATURDAY 4th APRIL 1970

A league debut for Peter Cormack, snapped up from Hibernian for £80,000 by Matt Gillies in order to paper over the self-harm caused by the sale of Joe Baker and the stark failure of Jim Baxter. He'd already been capped by Scotland and had amassed nearly 200 appearances for Hibs even though he was only 23. An attacking midfielder, it soon became apparent Cormack was too good for a fading Forest side. Once they'd been relegated from the top flight in 1972, he moved onto Bill Shankly's Liverpool for £110,000, enjoying four excellent years at Anfield before moving on to Bristol City. His career ended at Partick Thistle after a brief spell back at Hibernian, and he later had a pithy ten-day spell as manager of Cowdenbeath, during which the side didn't even play a game.

WEDNESDAY 5th APRIL 1990

A further example of the eccentric nature of Brian Clough. After losing 4-0 away at Goodison Park on live TV to Everton, Clough was asked by presenter Gary Newbon what had gone wrong with Forest (this being their sixth game without a win), to which Clough replied 'because they're just like you and me, Gary – a bunch of pansies', before kissing Newbon firmly on the cheek then walking off.

SATURDAY 5th APRIL 1930

A sad end to the career of Percy Barratt, Forest's much-lauded left-back of the late 1920s. Injured in a game at home to Grimsby Town in January 1929, Percy spent an entire year recuperating before playing again at home to Swansea Town, but this was to be his final appearance. A tough-tackling defender with a thunderbolt shot, Percy passed away in 1974.

SATURDAY 6th APRIL 1968

An awful day for Forest as they were taken apart by Wolverhampton Wanderers' Derek Dougan at Molineux in a 6-1 loss. The Irish schemer helped himself to a hat-trick, going on to score a further three just four days later in the UEFA Cup against Portuguese side Academica de Coimbra.

MONDAY 6th APRIL 1981

Robert Earnshaw was born in Mufulira, Zambia. Rescued from a nightmare spell at Derby County where he'd scored one goal in 22 games, Earnshaw was signed for Forest by Colin Calderwood in a £2.65 million deal. Earnshaw gained fame as the answer to the pub quiz standard 'Who is the only player to have scored hat-tricks in all four divisions of the Football League, the FA Cup, the League Cup and in an international?'

SATURDAY 7th APRIL 1934

Cyril Stocks made his final appearance for the club in an away game at Fulham which the Reds lost 3-1, marking the end of a decade's service mainly at inside-right. A Derbyshire man, Stocks played for South Normanton Colliery before linking up with Forest in 1924. He ended up making 257 appearances for the club, scoring 80 goals before joining Grantham.

SATURDAY 8th APRIL 1967

The City Ground hosted an epic FA Cup quarter-final tie between Forest and Everton. Having lost striker Joe Baker to injury within two minutes, Forest were 1-0 down when, just after the break, Andy Rankin couldn't hold Frank Wignall's shot and Moore pounced to slot the ball home. Forest took the lead with their next attack, Moore scoring a second with a screaming shot. Forest were well on top by this stage, but against the run of play Jimmy Husband scored his second with 12 minutes to go. Then came an incredible final minute – the ball fell to Moore in the area; he shot, but hit Ray Wilson, then shot again, but the ball hit Rankin and ballooned out. Miraculously, the ball fell kindly to Moore, who headed it goalwards, only for it to hit the crossbar. Yet again, the ball fell to Moore and this time his header ended up in the net.

SATURDAY 8th APRIL 2000

John Terry made his debut for Forest at home to Charlton Athletic, having been signed on loan by David Platt to boost a leaking Forest defence and to give the 19-year-old vital match experience. The defender played out the rest of the season in Forest's back four, with his enormous potential quite evident to all those who witnessed him there.

SATURDAY 9th APRIL 1898

The Town Ground hosted a Forest league match for the final time, with Bury the opponents in a 3-1 victory for the Reds. Having raised the necessary £3,000 to finance a move, for the 1898/99 season Forest would move a few hundred yards away at the opposite end of Trent Bridge, to the newly-built 'City Ground'. It was named in recognition of Nottingham's elevation to city status in 1897, even though the ground was actually positioned outside the city boundary.

SATURDAY 9th APRIL 1988

There was no FA Cup joy for Brian Clough today as his Forest side were beaten 2-1 at Hillsborough by Liverpool in the semi-final. John Aldridge did the main damage for Liverpool, scoring after 13 and 52 minutes, with Nigel Clough pulling one back to no avail in the 67th minute.

SUNDAY 9th APRIL 1989

Brian Clough got his hands on silverware for the first time in almost a decade, as Forest defeated Luton Town in the Littlewoods Cup final at Wembley. It was Forest's first trophy since winning the European Cup in 1980. They began the match nervously despite being favourites, and it was Luton who drew first blood, taking the lead ten minutes before half-time with a header from Mick Harford. This awoke the slumbering Reds and, after a Lee Chapman goal was disallowed, they equalised two minutes into the second half when Les Sealey felled Steve Hodge and Nigel Clough converted the penalty. From that point onwards Forest took full control and put the game beyond the Hatters with further goals from Neil Webb and Clough again. Forest: Sutton, Laws, Pearce, Walker, Wilson, Hodge, Gaynor, Webb, Clough, Chapman, Parker.

SATURDAY 10th APRIL 1937

A humiliating experience for the Reds at Blackburn Rovers as they suffered their heaviest-ever league defeat, losing 9-1. Billy Guest scored four for Rovers; indeed, Rovers players actually scored all ten goals as Forest's sole effort was an own goal from Bob Pryde.

MONDAY 11th APRIL 1898

In a dress rehearsal for the forthcoming FA Cup final, Forest went to Derby County for a league game and were soundly beaten 5-0, with Rams legend Steve Bloomer netting a hat-trick.

WEDNESDAY 11th APRIL 1979

One of those great nights of European football, as Forest took on the West German champions Cologne in a first leg quarter-final tie at a muddy City Ground. After only six minutes Roger van Gool put Cologne ahead when he was allowed space for a shot Peter Shilton could only touch into the net. Things got even worse after 20 minutes when, on a breakaway, van Gool passed to an unmarked Dieter Muller in front of an open goal to make it 2-0. Garry Birtles pulled one back just before the half-hour mark with a header set up by David Needham. Then, nearly ten minutes into the second half, a Robertson chip was knocked down by Birtles to Ian Bowyer, who fired past Harald Schumacher. Ten minutes later Forest went ahead, Robertson's flying header converting Birtles' excellent centre. Just as Forest were counting themselves lucky at taking a lead to West Germany, Cologne substitute Yashiko Okudera received and controlled the ball with his first touch before firing it under Shilton. An incredible game, and one that inspired the unforgettable headline 'Forest Sunk By Jap Sub'.

MONDAY 12th APRIL 1909

The final appearance for Forest, at home to Bury, by their custodian of a decade's worth of service, James Henry 'Harry' Linacre. The nephew of Forest's footballing brothers Frank and Fred Forman, Harry was born, like them, in Aston-on-Trent, Derbyshire, and also began his career at Derby County. He moved to Forest in 1899 and became the Reds' regular man between the posts for ten years, amassing more than 300 appearances and two England caps, in 1905 against Wales and Scotland. Harry passed away in 1957.

SUNDAY 12th APRIL 1992

In what turned out to be Brian Clough's final appearance at Wembley and his final major cup final as a manager, Forest were felled in a tame Rumbelows Cup final against Alex Ferguson's Manchester United. Forest offered very little throughout the entire game and went down to Brian McClair's 14th minute goal. Forest: Marriott, Charles (Laws), Williams, Walker, Wassall, Keane, Crosby, Gemmill, Clough, Sheringham, Black.

FRIDAY 13th APRIL 1877

One of Forest's all-time legends, striker Grenville Morris, was born today in Builth Wells, Powys, Wales. Morris was signed from Swindon Town in 1898 for £200 after scoring 44 goals in 50 games, maintaining a prolific scoring rate for his new club in a 14-year career totalling a record 217 goals. Morris also played regularly for Wales, winning 21 caps and scoring nine times. He lived to see Forest win the FA Cup in 1959, passing away in November of that year.

SATURDAY 13th APRIL 1907

The Reds secured promotion from the Second Division and back into the top flight after only one year of second tier football. They beat West Bromwich Albion 3-1 at home with goals from 'Knocker' West, Arthur Green and Tom Marrison.

SUNDAY 14th APRIL 1991

Brian Clough's ambition to win the complete set of domestic trophies came one step closer as Forest reached the FA Cup final thanks to a 4-0 victory over West Ham United in the semi-final at Villa Park. A close and keenly-contested game was turned on its head after 26 minutes when referee Keith Hackett rather harshly sent off Hammers' defender Tony Gale for sending Gary Crosby tumbling in a challenge. The young Forest side's fluent and speedy football tired the ten men of their opponents and, once Crosby had put the Reds ahead on 49, the boys in claret and blue understandably capitulated. Further goals by Roy Keane, Stuart Pearce and Gary Charles cemented the Hammers' gloom. Forest were off to Wembley for their first FA Cup final since 1959, where Tottenham awaited, having seen off rivals Arsenal in the other semi-final.

SATURDAY 15th APRIL 1911

Forest completed a miserable season as they finished bottom of the First Division and were relegated. They lost their final match at Bristol City 5-1, completing an awful sequence of 13 league games without a win, their last victory being at home to Liverpool on the 21st of January.

SATURDAY 16th APRIL 1892

A champion day for Forest as they beat Small Heath (a club now better known as Birmingham City) 2-1 away to secure first place in the Football Alliance. Set up in 1889 as a Midlands rival to the more northern Football League, Forest had been founder members of the Alliance, finishing second-bottom in 1890 and fifth in 1891. This was the last year of the Alliance, as at the end of the season it merged with the newly two-tiered Football League, although Forest's success meant they leapfrogged straight into Division One.

SATURDAY 16th APRIL 1898

Forest got their hands on a major piece of silverware for the first time in their history by defeating the fancied Derby County in the FA Cup final at Crystal Palace. In a rather dour final, Forest took the lead after 19 minutes. Alf Spouncer was fouled on the byline by Jack Cox, and Billy Wragg's resultant free kick fell to Arthur Capes, whose low shot beat Jack Fryer. The Rams equalised 12 minutes later when Steve Bloomer headed in from Joe Leiper's free kick. The Reds re-took the lead three minutes from the break through Capes' second, as Fryer failed to hold a shot from Chas Richards. The second half belonged to Derby, mainly due to an injury to Wragg which saw him consigned to limping along the left wing. Forest's defence held out superbly, and the cup was on its way to Nottingham when skipper John McPherson fired home from John Boag's weak headed clearance with four minutes remaining. Forest: Allsop, Ritchie, Scott, Frank Forman, McPherson, Wragg, McInnes, Richards, Bennow, Capes, Spouncer. Sourly, Forest are famously pictured with the 1898 FA Cup wearing Derby's kit! The photographer of the day thought Derby's white shirts and black shorts would look better on film than Forest's usual kit of red shirts and dark blue shorts!

SATURDAY 17th APRIL 1954

Forest completed their home fixtures with a 1-0 defeat to Blackburn Rovers, which was their first home league defeat of the season. The Reds missed out on promotion by four points, finishing fourth behind Leicester City, Everton and Rovers.

SUNDAY 17th APRIL 1988

The Reds won the Football League Centenary Festival at Wembley, beating Sheffield Wednesday 3-2 on penalties after the clubs had drudged out a 0-0 draw.

SATURDAY 18th APRIL 1925

West Bromwich Albion were the visitors to the City Ground, chasing Huddersfield Town in the title race. Forest were in their own battle to avoid relegation from the top flight after two near-misses in 1922/23 and 1923/24 (finishing one place above the relegation zone on each occasion). This time there was to be no lucky escape for lacklustre Forest, as a Joe Carter goal after a quarter of an hour sent them down to the second flight along with Preston North End. The win wasn't sufficient for the Baggies either, as Huddersfield pipped them to top spot.

TUESDAY 19th APRIL 1960

A final appearance today for the long-serving Gerald Shannon 'Geoff' Thomas in a 0-0 draw at home against Wolves after 16 years at the club. The Derby-born defender joined Forest during World War II, taking time to establish himself in the team. He managed it during the promotion campaign of 1950/51, but was always unlucky with injuries and fell in and out of favour during his time at the club, battling with the likes of Jack Hutchinson and Bill Whare for a full-back place. Thomas finally became first-choice pick between 1954 and 1958, unluckily losing his place to Joe McDonald right at the wrong moment, as McDonald played in the 1959 FA Cup final with Thomas on the bench. Thomas left in 1960 after more than 400 games for the Reds, becoming player-manager of Bourne Town and a greengrocer in Woodthorpe once his playing days were over.

MONDAY 20th APRIL 1964

A crowd of 6,330 turned up at the City Ground to see the Reds take on the touring New Zealand national team. Forest won rather handsomely, 8-0, with goals from Frank Wignall (3), Colin Addison (2), Alan Hinton (2) and Ian Storey-Moore. This was the worst result of New Zealand's short tour – they also lost 4-0 to an England FA XI, 4-1 to England Amateurs and 5-1 to Swindon Town.

THURSDAY 20th APRIL 1978

Forest's Kenny Burns was named the Sportswriters' Player of the Year, the first Forest player to be given this accolade. It marked the end of a significant journey for the Scot, signed in the summer of 1978 after an excellent season as a striker for Birmingham City only to be told he'd be partnering Larry Lloyd in defence. Severely criticised by Brian Clough after a headless display in that season's worst defeat (3-0 at Arsenal, during which Burns had been caught on camera head-butting Richie Powling), Burns had matured sufficiently to temper the more rambunctious aspects of his play, and his shrewd defending was rewarded with this honour.

SATURDAY 20th APRIL 1991

During a magnificent run of form, Forest took on Chelsea at the City Ground and beat them 7-0 with a brand of free-flowing and frenetic football which utterly bamboozled Chelsea's defence. The goalscorers were Roy Keane (2), Stuart Pearce (2), Garry Parker, Ian Woan and Gary Crosby. Amazingly, both strikers – Nigel Clough and Lee Glover – failed to score, although both played a full part in the dazzling victory.

SATURDAY 21st APRIL 1909

Forest gained their record home win, a mere 12-0 mauling of Leicester Fosse. Fosse were rock-bottom of Division One at the time, but this result was a massive shock as Forest were part of an immense 14-team melee to avoid the drop. An investigation was launched, and Fosse goalkeeper Horace Bailey admitted most of the Leicester players had spent the previous two days celebrating the marriage of inside-left Billy Turner. The result was allowed to stand, and the Forest scorers were Grenville Morris (2), Alf Spouncer (3), Bill Hooper (3), 'Knocker' West (3) and Edwin Hughes.

SATURDAY 21st APRIL 1979

In a game at St Andrew's, Forest beat Birmingham City 2-0 with goals from Garry Birtles and John Robertson, sending the Blues out of the top flight for the first time since 1972.

SATURDAY 22nd APRIL 1961

Brian Grant became Forest's youngest-ever league player, making his debut in a 2-2 home draw against Leicester City eight days shy of his 18th birthday. The Scottish full-back would play 22 games for the Reds before becoming Brian Clough's first signing at Hartlepool United in 1965.

SATURDAY 22nd APRIL 1978

Forest were crowned champions of the Football League for the first time in their history. Tired by an exhausting programme which saw them attack three trophies (winning two of them), Forest limped to a title secured with a 0-0 draw at Coventry City with four games to go. They would eventually finish clear in the top spot, seven points ahead of second-placed Liverpool, having only lost three games and conceded 24 goals all season. 'Our aim was to qualify for Europe,' said a delighted Peter Taylor. 'When we signed Peter Shilton, the best goalkeeper in the world, I knew we had a great chance to win the title.'

SATURDAY 23rd APRIL 1960

Johnny Quigley got the third goal in a 3-0 victory over Newcastle United, scoring Forest's 1,000th league goal. The other scorers were Geoff Vowden and Billy Gray.

WEDNESDAY 23rd APRIL 1980

The fairytale showed no sign of coming to an end as Forest reached the final of the European Cup for the second season in succession. Holding a 2-0 lead over Dutch champions Ajax from the first leg, a Kenny Burns-led defensive performance saw Forest hold out, even though they conceded a 65th minute goal to Soren Lerby. Forest's opponents in the final were German side Hamburg, who came back from a 2-0 first leg deficit against Real Madrid to take the second leg with a magnificent 5-1 win.

SATURDAY 24th APRIL 1915

Forest were beaten 7-0 by Arsenal in what turned out to be the club's final game for more than four years as the First World War saw football suspended. Harry King scored four for the Gunners.

SATURDAY 24th APRIL 1999

News to gladden the hearts of the vast majority of Forest fans – manager Ron Atkinson was to retire at the end of the season. The announcement lessened the sting of the club's latest relegation from the top flight, suffered after a 2-0 defeat at Aston Villa.

SATURDAY 25th APRIL 1914

The Reds completed a miserable season with a 2-1 defeat at Stockport County, leaving Forest 20th in Division Two and bottom of the entire Football League.

TUESDAY 25th APRIL 1978

The oddness-quotient of Nottingham Forest winning the 1977/78 Division One championship is surpassed by an occurrence of even greater rarity – Frank Clark scoring a goal! It was something the full-back never achieved in 389 games with Newcastle United, and so far – after nearly 100 games – had failed to manage with Forest. Clark was named on the bench for Forest's trip to Portman Road to take on Ipswich, and was called on to replace Peter Withe. Instead of shuffling the side, Brian Clough told left-back Clark to play up front, and the emergency striker nudged in the only goal of his entire career after 77 minutes.

WEDNESDAY 25th APRIL 1979

Ian Bowyer, only in the side due to Trevor Francis' European ineligibility, headed Forest to victory in the second leg of their European Cup semi-final tie at Cologne, the first leg having finished 3-3. The Reds were thought to have no chance, so Cologne were understandably shell-shocked when a 65th minute John Robertson corner was headed expertly on by Garry Birtles for Bowyer to plant past Harald Schumacher. Forest would play Malmo in the final after the Swedish side beat Austria Vienna in the other semi-final.

WEDNESDAY 25th APRIL 1984

One of the worst and most unfair nights of Forest's history in a UEFA Cup semi-final defeat by Anderlecht. It turned out the Belgians had an extra man on their side in the shape of referee Guruceta Muro. Having won the first leg 2-0 at the City Ground, Forest were confident of progression to a possible all-English final with Tottenham, but went down 3-0 in highly suspicious circumstances. Firstly, Muro gave a penalty when Kenny Swain was adjudged to have fouled a player he was actually nowhere near. Then, with seconds to go, Paul Hart headed Forest into the final only for the referee to disallow the goal without stating why, awarding a free kick to the Belgians instead. Brian Clough had already successfully judged the referee had been 'bought' and ordered his disgruntled players to change and head home barely seconds after coming off the pitch. It took 13 years for the truth to come out – Anderlecht chairman Constant Vanden Stock had given the referee a 'loan' of one million francs (around £27,000) with a rather favourable repayment schedule. Muro died in a car crash in 1987, and Anderlecht were forced to come clean once unnamed parties had attempted to bribe the club upon discovering evidence of Stock's wrongdoings. Anderlecht were banned from European competition for a year, although the ban was overturned on appeal as the offences had taken place well over a decade ago. Various legal actions by Forest and the players involved on the night came to nothing, and all efforts for justice were dropped in 2002.

MONDAY 26th APRIL 1993

Forest would go into the 1993/94 season in an unfamiliar position – without Brian Clough occupying the manager's office, as he was forced to admit plans of his retirement after they were leaked to the press. Forest's forthcoming game with Sheffield United – which the bottom-placed Reds needed to win to stand any chance of remaining in the top flight – would be Clough's final game at the City Ground, bringing down the curtain on almost two decades of managerial highs (and infrequent lows), silverware, far more wins than losses, eccentricities and football in the manner it is supposed to be played. Clough may never have been the top football manager of all time, but he was certainly in the top one.

SATURDAY 26th APRIL 1998

Forest virtually returned to the Premiership after only one season away thanks to a victory over Reading at the City Ground, secured by a low drive from Chris Bart-Williams with three minutes to go of an extremely nervous performance. Knowing that only freak results could thwart their promotion chances, the Forest fans good-naturedly invaded the pitch at the end, parading prolific striker Pierre van Hooijdonk around the City Ground.

SATURDAY 27th APRIL 1957

Veteran striker Doug Lishman scored a hat-trick and Tommy Wilson the other goal as Forest defeated Sheffield United 4-0 at Bramall Lane to win promotion back to Division One. Forest would be playing top-flight football for the first time in 32 years.

SATURDAY 27th APRIL 1965

Bobby McKinlay completed his fifth successive ever-present season by playing in Forest's final game of the season, a 1-1 draw at Blackburn Rovers. Centre-half McKinlay had last missed a Forest match on the 22nd of April 1959, and would complete a run of 265 consecutive games on the 16th of October 1965 before missing the following week's game at home to Aston Villa.

SATURDAY 28th APRIL 1898

Forest played their last ever game at the Town Ground before they moved to their new headquarters at the City Ground. The visitors were Leicester Fosse in the 'Burford Cup' final, Forest winning 1-0 thanks to an Arthur Capes goal.

SATURDAY 28th APRIL 1906

George 'Tag' Needham made his debut for Forest in the final game of the season, a 4-1 defeat to Everton. The Shepshed-born player had signed from Shepshed Albion that term, and would become the club's omnipotent centre-half right up until the outbreak of the First World War. A strong and intelligent player, his career was curtailed by the war.

NIGEL JEMSON SHAPES TO SHOOT HOME THE ONLY GOAL IN THE LITTLEWOODS CUP FINAL BETWEEN FOREST AND OLDHAM ON 29TH APRIL 1990

SATURDAY 29th APRIL 1967

No FA Cup final for Forest this year, as they were defeated 2-1 at Hillsborough by Tottenham Hotspur. Missing talismanic striker Joe Baker through injury, manager Johnny Carey moved Ian Storey-Moore to inside-left with Alan Hinton on the wing. Jimmy Greaves – who scored a huge number of goals against Forest during his career – put Spurs ahead on the half-hour, with Frank Saul adding a second after 67 minutes. Forest pulled a goal back with 15 minutes to go when Terry Hennessey headed a Barry Lyons corner onto the underside of the bar, down and in. Tottenham packed their defence for the remaining quarter of an hour, winning and progressing to play Chelsea in the Wembley final, which they won 2-1.

SUNDAY 29th APRIL 1990

Forest stumbled to their latest piece of silverware, defeating second division Oldham Athletic 1-0 in the Littlewoods Cup final at Wembley. Nigel Jemson scored the only goal of a tight and largely forgettable game, forcing the ball past Andy Rhodes at the second attempt after meeting a through-ball from Nigel Clough. Forest: Sutton, Laws, Pearce, Walker, Chettle, Hodge, Crosby, Parker, Clough, Jemson, Carr.

SUNDAY 30th APRIL 1989

One of the most thrilling Wembley finals of all time saw Forest beat Everton 4-3 in the Full Members Cup final. A sadly pointless competition sponsored by Simod and designed to somehow compensate for the ban of English clubs in European competition, this was Forest's second year of entry and their first final. Everton scored first via Tony Cottee, with Garry Parker equalising for the Reds. Everton led again, this time through Graeme Sharp, but Parker equalised again with a superb goal as he ran from his own half before beating Neville Southall. In extra time, Lee Chapman put Forest ahead for the first time with a fine shot, only for Cottee's second to level matters again. With penalties looming, Chapman was on hand to toe-poke home Franz Carr's cross. Forest: Sutton, Laws, Pearce, Walker, Wilson, Hodge, Gaynor, Webb, Clough, Chapman, Parker.

NOTTINGHAM FOREST
On This Day

MAY

SATURDAY 1st MAY 1926

A disappointing campaign which saw Forest finish 17th in the Second Division ended with a disappointing result, losing 8-3 at Oldham Athletic, for whom Albert Pynegar netted four times.

SATURDAY 1st MAY 1993

A tremendously emotional day as Brian Clough bowed out from the City Ground with a 2-0 loss to Sheffield United which saw Forest back where Old Big Ed found them – in the second flight. Anything but victory would have seen Forest relegated and, when Glyn Hodges put United ahead on the half-hour, the writing was on the wall. Brian Gayle's second, after 73 minutes, seemed largely immaterial, as Forest couldn't find the inspiration to pull themselves back into the game. The match concluded with both sets of supporters chanting Brian Clough's name after a grisly end to a brilliant managerial career.

SATURDAY 2nd MAY 1951

The Reds beat Newport County 2-1 at the City Ground thanks to a Colin Collindridge penalty and a Tommy Capel strike. In doing so, they secured promotion back to the second flight after two seasons in Division Three (South).

SATURDAY 2nd MAY 1959

The most glorious day in the club's history so far, as they defeated Luton Town 2-1 at Wembley, allowing skipper Jack Burkitt to receive the FA Cup from the Queen. In a thrilling game, Forest looked well on the way to victory after Roy Dwight had given them the lead after ten minutes, one which Tommy Wilson doubled just four minutes later. Tragedy struck after 33 minutes when Roy Dwight broke his leg in a collision with Brendan McNally, meaning Forest would have to play the last hour a man short. The extra man handed Luton the ascendancy and they pulled one back in the 66th minute via Derek Pacey. Despite losing Bill Whare to cramp for the final ten minutes, Forest clung on for victory. Forest: Thomson, Whare, McDonald, Whitefoot, McKinlay, Burkitt, Dwight, Quigley, Wilson, Gray, Imlach.

FRIDAY 3rd MAY 1991

Brian Clough returned from holiday to find that Archie Gemmill's reserve side had thrown away the Central League title, losing three out of their final four. Maddened, Clough suspended Gemmill until further notice.

SATURDAY 3rd MAY 1997

The Reds limped out of the top flight, drawing 1-1 at home to Wimbledon. It was also the final ever game in a Forest shirt for heroic left-back and temporary caretaker manager Stuart Pearce, who was given a free transfer to Newcastle United in the summer.

SATURDAY 3rd MAY 2008

Colin Calderwood saw his side end their exile in the third tier today with a 3-2 victory over Yeovil. Goals by Julian Bennett, Kris Commons and Lewis McGugan had given Forest a healthy 3-1 lead before a late Andy Kirk goal bequeathed the Reds a nervous final 15 minutes. Cheltenham Town's win over Doncaster Rovers kept Rovers down. This had been a most unexpected promotion campaign as Forest had been 11 points behind then second-placed Carlisle United at the beginning of April.

SATURDAY 4th MAY 1985

Forest's longest-serving player, Bryn Gunn, made his final appearance in a 1-1 home draw with Watford, a game which also saw Nigel Clough score his first senior goal. Gunn had made his debut way back in 1975 as a 17-year-old, but was never rated highly enough by Clough or Taylor to be given a decent run in the side, amassing only 161 games in 11 seasons. Gunn went on to play for Peterborough and Chesterfield. His daughter, Jenny, became an international cricketer for England.

SATURDAY 5th MAY 1990

Sheffield Wednesday surrendered their top-flight status with a meek display at Hillsborough, losing 3-0 to Forest via two goals from Stuart Pearce and one from Nigel Jemson. Luton Town's victory over Derby saw them survive instead of the Owls.

THURSDAY 6th MAY 1982

In a surprise announcement, Peter Taylor retired from football and resigned his post as Forest's assistant manager and Brian Clough's right-hand man, a position he had held for almost six amazingly successful years at Forest. Taylor's retirement would last just six months before he returned to the place he never wanted to leave, the Baseball Ground, as Derby County's full-time manager. This was one half of the cause of the rift between Clough and Taylor, the other being Taylor's acquisition of John Robertson in 1983. Taylor would not make a success of things at Derby, being unable to prevent the cash-strapped club from sliding into the third tier at the end of the 1983/84 season. He permanently retired from football at that point.

SATURDAY 7th MAY 1938

In the Reds' tightest-ever relegation battle, Forest drew 2-2 at Barnsley on the final day of the season to secure their Division Two status at the expense of the Tykes. Dave 'Boy' Martin had given Forest the lead early doors only for Beaumont Asquith to equalise. Barnsley went ahead in farcical circumstances when, having caught a fierce drive from Bert Barlow, Forest keeper Percy Ashton bounced the ball behind his own goal-line. With barely five minutes to go, Barnsley keeper Cliff Binns collected a Reg Trim cross, only to be barged across the goal-line by Martin. The goal was given and Forest survived with a goal average of 0.783 compared to Barnsley's 0.781 – a mere two-thousandths of a goal. Binns was so devastated at the nature of the goal that he had to be led from the field with his head in his hands.

SUNDAY 7th MAY 1989

Forest played their expected role as fall guys in the replayed FA Cup semi-final at Old Trafford, three weeks after the Hillsborough disaster. The Reds lost 3-1, John Aldridge scoring twice and Brian Laws putting through his own net. Aldridge scored first before Neil Webb restored parity for the Reds on 34. Aldridge grabbed his second after 59 minutes, then caused consternation on a sombre occasion by ruffling Brian Laws' hair when the defender scored an own goal in the 72nd minute. The striker later admitted his regret, claiming the moment had got the better of him.

THURSDAY 8th MAY 1997

Caretaker general manager Dave Bassett was given the role of team manager for the 1997/98 season, following the departure of Stuart Pearce to Newcastle United.

MONDAY 9th MAY 1960

John Winfield signed professional forms for Forest. Born in Draycott, Derbyshire on the 28th February 1943, Winfield originally came to the club as a promising half-back. Despite making several appearances there in the early 1960s, he dropped out of favour until 1966 due to the emergence of Henry Newton before re-establishing himself as a left-back, forming a long-lasting partnership with Peter Hindley and supporting Ian Storey-Moore on the wing. Winfield decided to join Peterborough United, managed by his former team-mate John Barnwell, at the end of the 1973/74 season, although injury forced his retirement after just 11 appearances. John was a familiar face at his newsagents in Nottingham's Victoria Centre for many years.

WEDNESDAY 9th MAY 1979

Forest beat Manchester City at the City Ground 3-1 to complete two entire seasons without a home defeat. The scorers were Garry Birtles, Ian Bowyer and Tony Woodcock, with Larry Lloyd scoring an own goal for City. Forest's last home defeat was on April 23rd 1977, against Cardiff City in the Second Division.

FRIDAY 10th MAY 1963

Legendary left-winger Ian Storey-Moore was given his debut – appropriately for the Ipswich-born midfielder, against Ipswich Town at the City Ground. Moore wore the number 11 shirt in a 2-1 victory, with Len Julians and an own goal by Ipswich goalie Roy Bailey providing the Reds' goals. Roy Stephenson replied for Town.

SUNDAY 10th MAY 1981

Forest returned to the scene of one of their greatest triumphs, the Santiago Bernabeu, where they had lifted the European Cup a year earlier by beating Hamburg. This time Forest lost 2-0 to Real Madrid in a friendly.

TUESDAY 11th MAY 2010

The Reds came unstuck during their latest attempt to return to the top flight after a gap of more than a decade, losing 4-3 in the second leg of their play-off semi-final against Blackpool. Trailing 2-1 from the first game despite having had an early lead via a sublime Chris Cohen strike, Rob Earnshaw levelled matters after only seven minutes. DJ Campbell put Blackpool back ahead after 56, but Earnshaw's second of the night in the 66th made the aggregate score 3-3. Blackpool edged ahead again six minutes later through sub Stephen Dobbie, and then tiring Forest seemed to freeze as Ian Holloway's men took full advantage, racing into an unassailable lead via two quick goals from Campbell to complete his hat-trick. This gave the Seasiders a 6-3 advantage, barely dented by Dele Adebola's late consolation. While Forest were left to rue what could have been, Blackpool went on to the promised land of the Premiership, beating Cardiff City 3-2 at Wembley.

WEDNESDAY 12th MAY 1993

Ex-Forest left-back Frank Clark was appointed the manager of Nottingham Forest, succeeding Brian Clough. Nominated by Clough himself, Clark had spent nine rather tame years as manager of Leyton Orient before a move upstairs in 1991. Rumour had it that Wycombe boss Martin O'Neill was approached first, with Clark suggested as general manager, but O'Neill turned this down to be his own man. Clark would succeed in his initial task of lifting Forest back into the top flight on his first attempt, guiding them into a third-place finish in the Premiership in 1994/95. He lost his way severely in 1996/97, resigning shortly before Christmas.

SATURDAY 13th MAY 1995

The final appearance for Forest by lethal marksman Stan 'The Man' Collymore in a 2-2 home draw with Wimbledon. Unusually, he failed to score, but the hottest property in football had scored a remarkable 45 goals in only 78 games for the Reds. He moved to Liverpool for a British record £8.5 million in the summer (see June 17th).

SATURDAY 14th MAY 1977

Forest were as good as promoted back to the First Division in only Brian Clough's second season in charge at the City Ground. Having completed their league programme a week earlier, Forest were second favourites to gain promotion behind Ian Greaves' Bolton Wanderers, who were four points behind but still had three games to play. All looked good for the Trotters as they beat Cardiff City 2-1 on the 10th, but then they took on already-promoted Wolverhampton Wanderers at Burnden Park, unexpectedly losing 1-0. This left them with the rather Herculean task of needing to beat Bristol Rovers 13-0 in their final game to overhaul Forest on goal difference.

SATURDAY 15th MAY 1982

Exciting young striker Peter Davenport announced himself to the footballing world with a hat-trick in a game against Ipswich Town at Portman Road in only his fifth appearance for the club. Given his chance by Brian Clough at the end of the insipid 1981/82 season, following the failure of Justin Fashanu, the Liverpudlian would go on to score 59 goals for Forest in 147 appearances before a £750,000 transfer to Manchester United in March 1986.

THURSDAY 15th MAY 2003

The Reds got their first taste of what would become an unfortunate habit for them – capitulation in the play-offs. Having finished sixth in Division One under the guidance of Paul Hart, Forest took on Sheffield United in the semi-final. Having drawn 1-1 in the first leg at the City Ground (in which Michael Dawson was sent off for a high tackle on Steve Kabba), they put themselves in an excellent position by taking a 2-0 lead at Bramall Lane thanks to goals from David Johnson and Andy Reid. Things soon fell apart in the second leg, though, as Neil Warnock's side scored the two goals they needed to take the tie into extra time via Michael Brown and Steve Kabba, then raced into a 4-2 lead on the night with goals from Paul Peschisolido and a Des Walker own goal. Rob Page put through his own net to give Forest forlorn hope with barely a minute to go, but it was not to be. United would go on to lose the final to Wolverhampton Wanderers.

FRIDAY 16th MAY 1987

Shocking news from the City Ground as long-serving pair Garry Birtles and Ian Bowyer were handed free transfers. Birtles would be snapped up by Notts County, and Bowyer joined Hereford United as player-manager. With Gary Mills soon out of the club as well, all Forest's links with their glory days of the twin European Cup wins over Malmo and Hamburg had now been severed.

SATURDAY 17th MAY 1919

Nottingham Forest won the Victory Shield, a war-time competition held between the winners of the Midlands Section and the Northern Section of what passed for league football during the First World War. Everton were Forest's opponents, the first leg at Goodison Park ending in a goalless draw, with the Toffeemen's Ernie Gault missing a penalty. Forest won the second leg, and hence the 'championship', thanks to a Noah Burton goal. Forest's team that day was Hardy; Bulling, Jones, Lowe, Wightman, Armstrong, Birch, Shea, Gibson, Burton, Martin. Walter Tinsley had played in the first leg in place of Tommy Gibson. The Shea in this line-up was the England international Danny Shea, who was a free-scoring forward for Blackburn Rovers prior to the war, going on to play for West Ham United, Fulham and Coventry City.

SATURDAY 17th MAY 1927

Forest's brilliant left-sided forward Charlie Jones was signed for Arsenal by Herbert Chapman for an impressive £4,800 – only £1,500 shy of the British record transfer fee at the time (Bob Kelly from Burnley to Sunderland). Born in Troedyrhiw, Merthyr Tydfil, on 12th December 1899, Charlie signed for Cardiff City after the First World War but only made one appearance for them before joining Stockport County for two years. He joined the Reds from Oldham Athletic in 1925, making exactly 100 league appearances for Forest with a tally of 22 goals. Upon moving to Highbury, Jones became first-choice for the Gunners during six excellent seasons of service before his retirement in 1934. Charlie would manage Notts County for a season in 1934/35, when they finished bottom of Division Two, and also played eight times for Wales. He passed away in April 1966.

DEJECTED SKIPPER STUART PEARCE WALKS OFF AT THE END OF THE 1991 FA CUP FINAL, WHICH TOTTENHAM BEAT THE REDS 2-1, ON 18TH MAY 1991

FRIDAY 18th MAY 1979

Forest concluded the 1978/79 season with a surprise 1-0 win at West Bromwich Albion courtesy of a Trevor Francis goal eight minutes from time. This victory meant Forest clinched the runners-up spot by finishing one place ahead of the Baggies, although they were still a hefty eight points behind champions Liverpool.

SATURDAY 18th MAY 1991

Brian Clough's sole FA Cup final ended in disappointment as Forest were defeated 2-1 by Tottenham Hotspur at Wembley Stadium. For this game, Clough remained faithful with the side which had played so well in the league in the previous weeks, meaning places for youngsters Gary Charles, Lee Glover and Ian Woan in preference to the more experienced Brian Laws, Nigel Jemson and Steve Hodge. This was billed to be Spurs midfielder Paul Gascoigne's final, being his last appearance in a Spurs shirt before an £8 million move to Italian side Lazio. Gascoigne certainly made his mark with two awful fouls on Garry Parker and Gary Charles, the latter punished with a free kick after 15 minutes from which Stuart Pearce fired Forest ahead (although referee Roger Milford missed Lee Glover pushing Gary Mabbutt out of the way of Pearce's strike). Gascoigne could and perhaps should have been sent off for a combination of these two fouls (or even either individually), and had damaged knee ligaments during his foul on Charles, and swiftly following Pearce's goal had to be stretchered off, his place being taken by Nayim. On 26 Gary Lineker netted for Spurs, only for the goal to be mistakenly chalked off for offside, then on 32 Lineker was brought down in the box by Mark Crossley, only for 'Big Norm' to save the resultant penalty. What didn't seem to be Spurs' day turned on 54 when Paul Stewart stroked the ball neatly home from Paul Allen's pass through a crowd of converging Forest players. As the game moved into extra time Tottenham clearly became the ascendant team, and they took the lead on 94 when Des Walker headed Paul Stewart's flick from Nayim's corner into his own net. Forest were exhausted and outplayed and there was no way back for them, so it was Tottenham skipper Gary Mabbutt and not Stuart Pearce who went on to lift the trophy. Forest: Crossley, Charles, Pearce, Walker, Chettle, Keane, Crosby, Parker, Clough, Glover (Laws), Woan (Hodge).

FRIDAY 18th MAY 2007

Yet more play-off embarrassment for Forest as Yeovil Town beat them 5-2 at the City Ground to complete a remarkable turnaround, Forest having beaten the Glovers 2-0 at Huish Park a week previously. At 1-1 with ten minutes to go Yeovil needed two goals to force extra time, and an Alan Wright own goal, followed by one from the experienced Marcus Stewart, saw them achieve just that. Things got even worse for Forest when David Prutton was sent off and Lee Morris added another goal. Gary Holt provided a little relief on 93 to make the tie 4-4 on aggregate, but Yeovil had the last laugh. Arron Davies' second goal and winner came on 109 minutes.

FRIDAY 19th MAY 1905

The players of Nottingham Forest left Nottingham to embark on a tour of South America for games against some of the top sides of Uruguay and Argentina. The voyage was expected to take three weeks just to reach Montevideo.

TUESDAY 19th MAY 1997

Forest left-back Stuart Pearce made his England debut at Wembley in a friendly against Brazil, becoming the 999th player to wear the three lions on his chest.

SATURDAY 20th MAY 1916

One of Forest's greatest-ever keepers, George Henry 'Harry' Walker, was born in Aysgarth. Harry played for Darlington and Portsmouth before World War II, winning an FA Cup winners' medal with Pompey in 1939. He came to Forest immediately after the war and wore the green jersey for almost a decade before injury forced his retirement in 1955. Harry passed away in January 1976.

SATURDAY 21st MAY 1949

Centre-half David Needham was born in Leicester. Needham would prove to be an excellent acquisition for Clough and Taylor, arriving from Queens Park Rangers for £150,000 in December 1977 to cover for the injured Larry Lloyd. Needham secured six caps for England 'B' during his time with the Reds, before moving on a free to Toronto Blizzard in the summer of 1982.

THURSDAY 22nd MAY 1980

Stan Bowles goes AWOL from Forest's post-season trip to Majorca, a move which cements the breakdown in relations between Clough and Bowles after Clough had refused to allow the ex-Queens Park Rangers man permission to play in John Robertson's testimonial. Bowles' actions would cost him a place in the 1980 European Cup final team.

SUNDAY 23rd MAY 1875

The birth of one of Forest's early true greats; Frank Forman, in Aston-on-Trent, Derbyshire. Frank played local football before moving to Beeston Town and then onto Derby County in March 1894, arriving at Forest in December of the same year. An outstanding half-back, Forman would serve Forest as a player for 11 seasons, as well as playing for England on nine occasions, captaining his country for the first time against Ireland on 22nd March 1902. With his brother Fred, Frank played in the 13-2 victory over Ireland in March 1899, the pair becoming the first brothers from the same club to represent England in the same match. Frank's last game for Forest came in January 1906, and he moved onto Forest's committee, a position he retained until his death on 4th December 1961. Frank later went into business as a building contractor with his nephew, the ex-Forest custodian Harry Linacre.

WEDNESDAY 24th MAY 1978

Peter Shilton won the 25th cap of his international career for England in a friendly at Wembley against Hungary. Despite the brilliance of his season with Forest, this was only Shilton's second cap while with the club, and only the fourth he'd won since April 1975, the main reason for Shilton's recent paucity of caps being Don Revie's preference for Liverpool goalkeeper Ray Clemence. Shilton would win a further century of caps for England before his retirement from international football after the 1990 World Cup.

SATURDAY 25th MAY 1991

A rare taste for international success for England as a side containing three Forest players in Stuart Pearce, Des Walker and Nigel Clough held Argentina to a 2-2 draw to win the friendly 'Challenge Cup'. They had beaten the other entrants, USSR, 3-1 four days beforehand.

SUNDAY 26th MAY 1991

Forest splashed out some of the cash gathered from the club's eventually unsuccessful FA Cup campaign in signing defender Carl Tiler from Barnsley for £1.4 million. It never really worked out for Tiler at the City Ground – a succession of niggly injuries spoilt 1991/92 for him, and 1992/93 was a disaster for the club all round. Tiler was sold by Frank Clark to Aston Villa for £750,000 in October 1995.

SUNDAY 27th MAY 1984

Forest commenced a post-season tour of Australia with a game against Western Australia at the Lake Manger Velodrome, Perth. The Reds won the game 4-1 with goals by Peter Davenport, Garry Birtles, Ian Bowyer and Gary Mills.

WEDNESDAY 28th MAY 1980

Forest enjoyed another superb night of European success, beating Hamburg to retain the European Cup. Robbed of playmakers Trevor Francis (through injury) and Stan Bowles (a dispute), Clough sent his team out at the Santiago Bernabeu to defend, packing the midfield with five players (including Gary Mills who, at 17, became the youngest player ever to appear in a European Cup final) and leaving Garry Birtles alone up front. It didn't make for a memorable final, but it did the job, thwarting a Hamburg forward line including the England international Kevin Keegan. John Robertson scored the vital goal after 19 minutes with a precise shot from outside the area, and the Forest defence conspired to survive everything the Germans could throw at them. Forest survived to become the first team to win Europe's highest prize more times than their domestic championship. Forest: Shilton, Anderson, Gray (Gunn), McGovern, Lloyd, Burns, O'Neill, Bowyer, Birtles, Mills (O'Hare), Robertson.

TUESDAY 28th MAY 1985

Forest announced the capture of Coventry City pair Ian Butterworth and Stuart Pearce for a fee of £240,000. Butterworth would disappoint at Forest, losing his place in the defence to the emerging Des Walker before being sold to Norwich City for £160,000 in October 1986. The transfer of the lesser-known Pearce would prove to be somewhat more successful for the club.

SUNDAY 29th MAY 1983

Forest appeared live on TV, but only for Canadian viewers as they took on Toronto Blizzard in a friendly in Canada. Forest lost the game 2-1, their goal coming from Peter Davenport.

WEDNESDAY 30th MAY 1979

Certainly the most memorable night in Forest's long history as they achieved the previously unthinkable – victory in the European Cup final. Forest's opponents were equally unfashionable Swedish team Malmo. Brian Clough caused a few raised eyebrows as regulars from the championship side Martin O'Neill and Archie Gemmill, both recovering from knocks, were omitted from the team despite both declaring themselves fit to play. They were replaced by Ian Bowyer and £1 million man Trevor Francis, who'd served a three-month ineligibility torment following his move in February. Malmo were forced to pick an injury-ravaged side (including only four of the permitted five substitutes) and lost captain Staffan Tapper (already nursing a broken toe) after 36 minutes. Just before half-time came the moment – John Robertson received the ball wide on the left, jinked into half a yard of clear space despite the attentions of two Malmo defenders, and crossed perfectly to find Trevor Francis gambling. Francis headed the ball home perfectly to give Forest a 1-0 lead. Malmo came into things in the second period but hadn't the invention or firepower to breach Peter Shilton's goal. Forest: Shilton,googgoo Anderson, Clark, McGovern, Lloyd, Burns, Francis, Bowyer, Birtles, Woodcock, Robertson.

TUESDAY 30th MAY 2006

Brief ex-Reds defender Colin Calderwood was prised from the hot-seat at Northampton Town to become the latest incumbent of the manager's chair at Forest, succeeding caretakers Barlow and McParland.

TUESDAY 31st MAY 1960

Striker Len Julians was snapped up from Arsenal, where he'd failed to establish himself since joining from Leyton Orient in December 1958. He never really became successful at Forest either, despite 25 goals in 61 games, and moved to Millwall in 1964.

NOTTINGHAM FOREST
On This Day

JUNE

SUNDAY 1st JUNE 1980

Forest told Barcelona that they would be willing to accept a fee of £1.5 million for striker Trevor Francis.

WEDNESDAY 2nd JUNE 1982

After 117 years of being run by a committee of 209 members, Nottingham Forest Football Club enjoyed their first day as a Public Limited Company.

SUNDAY 3rd JUNE 1984

Forest played Manchester United in a friendly at the Melbourne Cricket Ground, Australia. A crowd of 21,099 watched as United won 1-0 thanks to a Mark Hughes goal.

SATURDAY 3rd JUNE 1995

Stan Collymore made an uneventful England debut in a friendly against Japan at Wembley. For a player with an abundance of deadly talent, Collymore's England career would mirror his domestic career as a case of what could and should have been. He went on to make two further unremarkable appearances for his country – eight days later, as a substitute for Teddy Sheringham in a 3-1 defeat to Brazil, and then more than two years later for Glenn Hoddle's England in a World Cup qualifier against Moldova.

FRIDAY 4th JUNE 1993

The Clough connection at Forest was severed as Nigel followed his father out of the club, signing for Liverpool for a fee of £2.75 million after a decade at the City Ground. Initially a hit at Anfield, Clough's form would soon suffer, and the emergence of Robbie Fowler gave him limited first-team opportunities. He would play only ten games in the 1994/95 season, failing to score, and joined Manchester City in January 1996. He rejoined Forest briefly on loan in December 1996, scoring once in 13 league games. After a loan spell at Sheffield Wednesday he dropped out of league football at the end of the 1997/98 season, joining Burton Albion as player-manager at the age of 32. Clough retired from playing in 2006 and eventually helped guide Burton into the league before becoming manager of Derby County in 2009.

WEDNESDAY 5th JUNE 1985

Portsmouth's star midfield prospect Neil Webb seemed on his way to either Aston Villa or Queens Park Rangers until Brian Clough stepped in at the eleventh hour and persuaded him that the City Ground was a much more desirable destination for £250,000. A massively talented goalscoring midfielder, Webb was a precision passer who could sense playmaking opportunities in a snap, linking up magnificently with the similar, but more attack minded, Nigel Clough. For four years the pair remained the fulcrum of the Forest side until Alex Ferguson's chequebook tempted Webb away in July 1989, just as Forest seemed on the verge of something truly successful. Unfortunately for Webb he snapped his Achilles tendon whilst playing for England against Sweden and never seemed able to find his previous form after his recovery. He returned to Forest in November 1992 for £800,000 but a further injury curtailed any major influence he could have had and his career petered out. He retired in 1997.

WEDNESDAY 6th JUNE 1979

Good news and bad news for Forest's internationals in the European Championship qualifiers. Trevor Francis and Tony Woodcock both came on as subs in England's 3-0 win over Bulgaria in Sofia, but Martin O'Neill suffered a 4-0 defeat with Northern Ireland in Copenhagen against Denmark.

WEDNESDAY 7th JUNE 1978

Kenny Burns, Archie Gemmill and John Robertson all turned out for Scotland in their World Cup finals match against unfancied Iran at the Chateau Carreras Stadium in Cordoba, Argentina. Scotland could only draw 1-1, and needed a miracle in their final game against Holland to progress.

SATURDAY 8th JUNE 1991

A proud moment for Forest's Stuart Pearce as he captained England for the first time, in a friendly international against New Zealand in Wellington. Pearce would go on to skipper England ten times. He also scored in a 2-0 victory which marked the intenational debut of Reds right-back Gary Charles.

TUESDAY 8th JUNE 1982

Jurgen Rober left Forest for Bayer Leverkusen on the orders of his wife who, after a year in first Canada and then England, was feeling a little homesick for her native Germany. Signed from Calgary Boomers, Rober had been one of the few highlights of Forest's 1981/82 season, and at times it seemed Brian Clough had finally found a player to secure the void left by Archie Gemmill's departure in 1980. The ex-Werder Bremen midfielder would go on to be a successful manager in his homeland with, amongst others, VfL Wolfsburg and Borussia Dortmund.

WEDNESDAY 9th JUNE 2010

Brief ex-Red Neil Lennon was promoted from within to become the manager of Celtic. He became the second former Forest player to manage the Glasgow giants, after Martin O'Neill.

SATURDAY 10th JUNE 1950

Duncan McKenzie was born in Grimsby. The mercurial and sometimes eccentric forward would dally about Forest's first team for many a term before flowing in the 1973/74 season, when he scored 26 goals. The inevitable big-money move that followed was to Leeds United for a then-massive £240,000, signed by Brian Clough during his oh-so-brief stint at Elland Road. Despite success at Leeds, McKenzie had a nomadic career, with stints at Anderlecht, Everton, Chelsea, Blackburn Rovers, Tulsa Roughnecks and Chicago Sting.

SUNDAY 10th JUNE 1979

Forest had four players starting an England match for the first time in their history, in a friendly against Sweden at the Rasunda Football Stadium in Stockholm. Peter Shilton, Viv Anderson, Tony Woodcock and Trevor Francis took part in a quiet 0-0 draw.

SUNDAY 11th JUNE 1905

Having finally arrived in South America after leaving Nottingham three weeks ago (see 19th June), Forest played their first game against the Montevideo side Penarol. They won 6-1 with goals from Alf Spouncer (3), Tommy Niblo, Billy Shearman and an Isisarri own goal.

SUNDAY 11th JUNE 1978

The Reds' diminutive midfield schemer Archie Gemmill scored perhaps the most iconic goal in Scotland's international football history. In the 1978 World Cup finals Gemmill and co needed to win their final group game against fancied Holland by three clear goals to stay in the competition. Things were going better than expected with Scotland 2-1 up (one a Gemmill penalty). With about 20 minutes to go the ball fell to Gemmill just outside the area, and he skilfully jinked his way past two Dutch challenges before guiding the ball past Jan Jongbloed. A Johnny Rep goal three minutes later ended Scotland's hopes, though.

TUESDAY 12th JUNE 1990

Upon the recommendations of scout Noel McCabe, Brian Clough snapped up an unknown 18-year-old Irish midfielder named Roy Keane from Cobh Ramblers for an initial £10,000 (eventually rising to £47,000). Despite initially suffering from homesickness, Keane performed excellently in the club's youth team's tournament in Holland that summer, scoring the winning penalty in the shoot-out to decide the competition. Forest's coaching staff immediately knew they had a special player on their hands and Brian Clough thought nothing of handing the youngster a first-team league debut in the second game of the season at Anfield. Although Forest lost 2-0, Keane became an instant first-choice and never looked back.

WEDNESDAY 13th JUNE 2011

The recent managerial merry-go-round at Forest begins with the appointment of ex-England boss Steve McClaren as manager, following the surprise dismissal of Billy Davies three days earlier. McClaren would only last 111 days in charge before resigning; citing that the financial constraints placed upon him by owner Nigel Doughty meant he was unable to succeed. Doughty would resign as chairman the same day McClaren quit. McClaren managed to obtain eight points from his ten games as the reds' boss, and would later return to manage FC Twente in Holland. McClaren would be the first of several short-term appointments to the Forest red-hot-seat, and was followed by Steve Cotterill, Sean O'Driscoll and Alex McLeish before the return of Billy Davies in February 2013.

FRIDAY 14th JUNE 1991

Brian Clough was awarded the Order of the British Empire in the Queen's Birthday honours list. This confused many people, who thought it had been 'Brian Clough OBE' for years, the OBE of course standing for 'Old Big Ed'.

SUNDAY 15th JUNE 1980

Garry Birtles made his only competitive appearance for England, in the European Championships finals against Italy, but disappointed in an equally disappointing 0-0 draw and was substituted after 75 minutes.

FRIDAY 16th JUNE 1905

Forest continued their groundbreaking tour of South America with a friendly against the Argentinian side Rosario at the Plaza Jewell. The Reds ran out easy victors, winning 5-0 with goals from Tom Davies, Ben Shearman, Fred Lessons, Tommy Niblo and Alf Spouncer.

SATURDAY 17th JUNE 1995

Liverpool won the battle to sign Forest's lethal striker Stan Collymore, although they had to set a new British transfer record of £8.5 million to get their man. Despite maintaining a ratio of a goal every 2.5 games at Anfield, Stan later admitted he never really felt at ease with the culture at the club, and joined Aston Villa for £7 million in 1997. From that point on his well-publicised personal demons began to haunt him and his footballing career began to diminish, with brief spells over the next four years at Fulham, Leicester City, Bradford City and the Spanish side Real Oviedo, with whom he managed three goalless games before announcing his ridiculously premature retirement at the age of 30.

MONDAY 18th JUNE 1979

Veteran Jimmy Montgomery, possibly the most 'unknown' Forest player of Brian Clough's reign at the club, signed on a one-year deal from Birmingham City. The ex-Sunderland keeper's entire Forest career would consist of sitting on the bench in European Cup ties, although he did play one competitive match, the 1979 County Cup final against Notts County.

FRIDAY 18th JUNE 1993

Frank Clark stumped up the £1.7 million that Brian Clough was too reluctant to on Millwall's defender Colin Cooper. A terrific defender in ever sense of the word, Cooper would endear himself to the Forest faithful with his no-nonsense approach and thrilling runs from the back. Cooper won two England caps while at the club, and his sale back to hometown club Middlesbrough just as the 1998/99 season began, thanks to Dave Bassett and a 'gentlemen's agreement', came as both a shock and a massive kick in the teeth.

SATURDAY 19th JUNE 1987

Defender Courtney Huw 'Chris' Fairclough joined Tottenham Hotspur the day before for a fee later set by a tribunal at £387,000 after his contract at Forest expired. A classy defender, the loss would have been a huge blow had it not been eased by the emergence around the same time of Des Walker. Fairclough went on to Leeds United, where his defensive partnership with Chris Whyte helped the Peacocks to the 1991/92 league title, then played for Bolton Wanderers and Notts County before joining Forest's coaching staff in 2004. Chris' son, Jordan, was an apprentice at the club before his release in 2010.

SUNDAY 20th JUNE 2007

Nottingham Forest announced plans for a new 40,000 capacity (rising to 50,000 should the club manage to return to the top flight) stadium to be built in the southern outskirts of Nottingham. Plans were put on hold, however, in December 2010 upon England's failing to be awarded the hosting of the 2018 World Cup.

MONDAY 21st JUNE 1964

Dean Saunders was born in Swansea. The free-scoring striker ended up netting more than 200 career goals with 13 clubs including Liverpool and Aston Villa, as well as the Welsh national team. He almost joined Forest in September 1992 as the replacement for Teddy Sheringham, but Brian Clough refused to meet Saunders' wage demands. Saunders did eventually join the Reds in 1996 for £1.5 million, but found his first-team chances limited by the success of Pierre van Hooijdonk and Kevin Campbell as a front pairing. He left for Sheffield United on a free transfer in December 1997, and became the manager of Wrexham in October 2008.

THURSDAY 22nd JUNE 1905

Forest continued their tour of South America with an easy game over 'Britanicos', a team of British residents. The Reds ran out 13-1 winners, with Fred Lessons and Ben Shearman both scoring four goals. The other scorers were Alf Spouncer (2), Tom Davies, Tommy Niblo and a Charles Clifford penalty.

SATURDAY 22nd JUNE 1996

Stuart 'Psycho' Pearce exorcised some of the ghosts of his infamous Italia 90 penalty miss by scoring the third penalty in England's European Championships quarter-final shoot-out against Spain, after the match had finished goalless. His exuberant, sinew-straining celebrations after he'd fired the ball past Andoni Zubizarreta suggested he was more than slightly relieved about hitting the target.

WEDNESDAY 23rd JUNE 1954

Forest defender Steve Baines was born in Newark, Nottinghamshire. Steve would only play two first-team games for the Reds, in the 1972/73 season, before going on to a lengthy career in the lower divisions with Huddersfield Town, Bradford City, Walsall, Bury, Scunthorpe United and Chesterfield. He then achieved something only two previous ex-professionals had achieved before him by becoming a professional referee in the Football League.

WEDNESDAY 23rd JUNE 1993

Newly-installed manager Frank Clark again showed he didn't have the same qualms about splashing the cash that Brian Clough fell victim to in the last months of his reign by paying an initial £2 million for Southend United's exciting young striker Stan Collymore. The engorged fee marked quite an upturn in the value of the fiery forward, who had been released by Walsall and Wolverhampton Wanderers as a youngster, then signed by Crystal Palace (for whom he only managed one goal in what were largely substitute appearances) from Stafford Rangers for £100,000. He joined the Shrimpers for £150,000. After 15 goals in 30 games and a profit of £1.85 million, Southend were hardly complaining. Forty-five goals and a £6.5 million profit later, neither were Forest.

TUESDAY 24th JUNE 2008

Striker Grant Holt was sold to Shrewsbury Town for a rather meagre £170,000, completing a remarkable turnaround for the player who was voted Forest's Player of the Season in 2006/07. Holt ended up scoring 20 goals in 43 games for the Shrews in 2007/08, earning himself a trip back up the league ladder to Norwich City for around £400,000 at the end of that season.

SUNDAY 25th JUNE 1905

Touring Forest completed a 6-1 victory over Argentinian side Alumni, following up the previous day's 6-0 win over Rosario.

MONDAY 26th JUNE 1989

Young Irish midfielder John Sheridan was signed from Leeds United as a natural replacement for Neil Webb, now at Old Trafford. What should have been a case of a round peg fitting into a round hole turned out to be anything but, as Brian Clough would refuse to select Sheridan. He was on his way to Sheffield Wednesday by November.

MONDAY 27th JUNE 1966

Tommy Cavanagh was appointed as Forest's first-team coach. The Liverpudlian came to the club after a brief spell as manager of Brentford following a mundane playing career with, among others, Huddersfield Town and Doncaster Rovers. A popular figure, Tommy would remain coach throughout Forest's best pre-Clough years, until his departure in 1972 to join Tommy Docherty's ultimately successful campaign to partly return Manchester United to past glories. He left United in 1981, working at the FA School of Excellence at Lilleshall until he retired. Tommy passed away in March 2007.

THURSDAY 28th JUNE 1979

One in and one out for Forest. In came experienced midfielder Asa Hartford from Manchester City, a potential replacement for Archie Gemmill, for £450,000. Out went excellent young goalkeeper Chris Woods, who slipped down a division to sign for Queens Park Rangers for £235,000.

TUESDAY 29th JUNE 1999

The fractious relationship between Nottingham Forest and Pierre van Hooijdonk came to an end when the free-scoring Dutchman joined Vitesse Arnhem for £3.5 million. Infamous for his strike at the start of the 1998/99 season over Forest's alleged refusal to grant him a transfer and his dissatisfaction over the sales of Kevin Campbell and Colin Cooper and the refusal of the club to significantly strengthen their squad, van Hooijdonk's relationships with both team-mates and supporters had soured to the extent that his departure was utterly inevitable. He went on to tellingly-brief stints at Benfica, Fenerbahce, Breda and twice at Feyenoord, scoring goals at an extremely prolific rate wherever he went before calling it a day in 2007.

FRIDAY 30th JUNE 1995

Frank Clark used a large percentage of the cash generated by the sale of Stan Collymore to snap up two players – Arsenal striker Kevin Campbell and Sheffield Wednesday midfielder Chris Bart-Williams. Both players were already known to Clark, Campbell having been on loan at Orient in 1989 when Clark was manager (he was knocked back in an attempt to sign the 19-year-old after he'd scored nine goals in 16 games), Bart-Williams having begun his career under Clark at Brisbane Road before signing for Wednesday for £275,000 while only 17. Campbell, who cost £3 million, would suffer two injury-plagued years before blossoming in the promotion campaign of 97/98, earning himself a move to Turkish side Trabzonspor. Bart-Williams, the cheaper of the pair at £2.5 million, would prove effective in a number of positions including sweeper, until Forest's financial slide saw him leave for Charlton Athletic for free in December 2001.

TUESDAY 30th JUNE 2009

Paul Anderson's loan move from Liverpool to Forest was made permanent for a fee of £250,000. The young winger had completed a season on loan at the City Ground the previous term, playing 26 games and scoring twice. Having started his career at Hull City, Anderson had been snapped up and taken to Anfield as an 18-year-old, but failed to make the first team in three years there, spending the 2007/08 season on loan to Swansea City.

NOTTINGHAM FOREST
On This Day

JULY

THURSDAY 1st JULY 1999

Former England star David Platt was the surprise new appointment as manager of Nottingham Forest. After an illustrious career with Aston Villa, in Italy and with Arsenal, Platt failed as manager of one of his Italian clubs, Sampdoria, lacking the necessary qualifications (and experience) to manage in Serie A. Despite being bankrolled by the club and allowed to spend significant amounts on the likes of Salvatore Matrecano, Gianluca Petrachi, Ricky Scimeca and David Johnson, the club simply spent most of the period bouncing around mid-table during Platt's two seasons in charge. Platt was offered the position of manager of the England U21s at the end of the 2000/01 season and, being naturally ambitious, jumped at the chance. He paid the price for the side's failure to qualify for the 2004 European Championships, resurfacing in 2010 as first-team coach at Manchester City alongside former team-mate Roberto Mancini.

SUNDAY 2nd JULY 1905

Another huge victory for the Reds during their tour of South America, as they defeated an Argentinian League XI 9-1 at the Sociedad Sportiva. Fred Lessons nabbed his second four-goal haul of the tour, with other goals from Tommy Niblo (2), George Henderson, Sammy Timmins and Ben Shearman.

THURSDAY 3rd JULY 1997

Manager Dave Bassett got ready for the second tier following his side's relegation the previous term by signing Norwich City's combative midfielder Andy Johnson for £2 million. The Bristol-born player spent four years at the City Ground before a cut-price move to West Bromwich Albion, later playing for Leicester City and Barnsley.

WEDNESDAY 4th JULY 1990

Heartbreak for Forest pair Stuart Pearce and Des Walker as their dreams of a World Cup final appearance for England ended with defeat on penalties to West Germany. Of course, many England fans blamed Pearce's penalty – hit straight at Bodo Illgner – for the country's elimination, although Chris Waddle's was even worse.

FRIDAY 4th JULY 1997

More transfer dealings for Bassett as he snapped up Tranmere's hugely promising left-back Alan Rogers for £2 million. Rogers would become Forest's regular number three for four years, although he spent some time on the left side of midfield, a positional switch instigated during Ron Atkinson's brief time at the club.

MONDAY 5th JULY 2010

Forest's second-longest-serving player, James Perch, enjoyed an instant rise to the Premiership after his club had faltered in the play-offs by joining Newcastle United for an undisclosed fee. Perch had managed to amass more than 200 games for the Reds in seven years despite never really holding down a regular first-team place. His versatility – being able to appear on the right or centre of defence or midfield, proved a curse.

FRIDAY 6th JULY 1979

Left-back Frank Clark announced his retirement from football to take up the assistant manager's role under Ken Knighton at Sunderland. Released by Newcastle United in 1975 after 13 years of sterling service, Clark was handed an unbelievable swansong to his career by Brian Clough, although he missed much of the 1977/78 championship campaign through injury. Glory in the European Cup final of 1979 seemed an ideal way of Clark bringing the curtain down on his City Ground career, although of course he would return in 1993 to take up the reins recently relinquished by his former boss.

MONDAY 6th JULY 1987

The popular Dutch midfielder-defender Johnny Metgod left Forest for Tottenham Hotspur in a surprise deal, with the fee later decided at tribunal to be £250,000. Johnny had been signed from Real Madrid in the summer of 1984, and proved to be an instant hit with his strength, vision and expertise at free kicks. A hernia injury and the departure of the man who signed him, David Pleat, meant the move to White Hart Lane would not work out for him, and he moved to Feyenoord in 1988.

SATURDAY 7th JULY 1990

Ex-Reds keeper Peter Shilton ended his international career on 125 caps in the pointless third place play-off against hosts Italy at the 1990 World Cup finals.

TUESDAY 8th JULY 2008

Forest completed the signing of ex-Arsenal and Manchester United striker Andrew Cole, following his release from Sunderland after four days of negotiations. 'It's a dream come true. I always said that one day I would play for Forest,' said Nottingham-born Cole, who was first linked to the club 17 years beforehand, while Brian Clough was the manager. The dream swiftly turned into a nightmare, and Cole was released by mutual consent 11 appearances, no goals and a mere four months into his 12-month contract. He announced his retirement from football 11 days later.

FRIDAY 9th JULY 2010

Young winger Garath McCleary signed a new three-year contract with the club. Forest signed him from non-league Bromley in January 2008 after he'd impressed on trial. In 2011 he became Forest's record holder for substitute appearances.

TUESDAY 10th JULY 2012

Forest move into a new era, when the club is purchased by the Al-Hasawi family of Kuwait, the owners of Al-Quadisya Sports Club in their native country. The 2012/13 season promised to be an interesting one for Forest fans, and so it turned out...

TUESDAY 11th JULY 1978

The Reds may have felt slightly cheated as they learnt they would open their first-ever European Cup campaign with an excursion to Merseyside to take on holders Liverpool.

THURSDAY 12th JULY 2001

On the day that David Platt left the club's managerial position, Forest owner Nigel Doughty was quick to announce that Academy director Paul Hart would be the new Reds boss.

WEDNESDAY 13th JULY 1994

Manager Frank Clark pulled off one of the major transfer coups of the close season when he unexpectedly acquired the services of exciting young Dutch international Bryan Roy for his newly-promoted side. Upon deciding that he needed a player 'like Bryan Roy' to bolster his squad, Clark was amazed to find that Roy was available from his current side Foggia, and £2.9 million later Roy came to Nottingham. Despite being viewed as a left-winger, Clark eyed Roy as a companion to Stan Collymore, and the pair instantly gelled, sending Forest to a third place finish with 39 goals between them. Once Collymore had departed Roy became less effective, and he faded from the first-team picture completely before leaving for Hertha Berlin. His depature was sour, rather petulantly commenting that 'all Nottingham has is Robin Hood – and he's dead.' Roy would later play for NAC Breda before retiring in 2002, and he became a coach at Ajax Amsterdam.

WEDNESDAY 14th JULY 2004

Forest were defeated by DC United in a friendly at Washington's RFK Stadium, 4-3 on penalties, with the winning penalty coming from the boot of their ex-player, Ben Olsen. United, who included 15-year-old 'wonderkid' Freddy Adu in their line-up, took a ninth minute lead though Ezra Hendrickson before Andy Reid equalised for Forest just after the half hour. After no further goals the game was decided on spot-kicks, with Forest losing 4-3. Before the game the USA female champions Washington Freedom routed Nottingham Forest Ladies 8-0.

SATURDAY 15th JULY 2000

Forest wrapped up their short two-game tour of the USA with a 3-1 win over Jamaican side Harbor View in Miami. The Forest scorers were Gary Jones and Jack Lester with two. Forest had previously lost 3-2 to Miami Fusion three days earlier.

FRIDAY 16th JULY 1976

Peter Taylor resigned as manager of Brighton & Hove Albion to rejoin his old mucker Brian Clough as assistant manager of Forest.

MONDAY 16th JULY 2007

Forest snapped up Nottingham-born central defender Kelvin Wilson from Preston North End for £300,000. After starting his career at Meadow Lane, Wilson had joined Preston in March 2006 after an initial loan spell, but found it hard to break into their first team. He took a while to settle at Forest as well, but played the best football of his career during the 2009/10 failed play-off campaign. His relationship soured with the club the following term as constant speculation linked him with Celtic. The move came to fruition when he signed a pre-contract agreement with the Glasgow side in January 2011.

SATURDAY 17th JULY 1976

Sean Haslegrave was signed from Stoke City by Brian Clough (and the newly-installed Peter Taylor) for £50,000. Injuries and the resurgence of Martin O'Neill restricted Haslegrave to just seven games with Forest, and he moved to Preston in September 1977.

SUNDAY 17th JULY 1977

Forest paid a record fee of £150,000 for Birmingham City striker Kenny Burns. Glasgow-born Burns had begun his career as a defender with Glasgow Rangers, moving to Birmingham City in 1971 at the age of 17. In 1974 he converted to a striker following Bob Latchford's record-breaking transfer to Everton, moving up front with a huge amount of success. He ended the 1976/77 season as one of the First Division's leading goalscorers, hitting 19 goals. Shortly after Burns' signing Clough announced that the Scot would be converted back to a defender with Forest, replacing 'Sammy' Chapman who'd been given a free transfer to Notts County at the end of the promotion season. This re-conversion was an even greater success as Burns went on to become one of the game's classiest and most effective defenders. His partnership in the heart of the Reds defence with the equally gargantuan Larry Lloyd became legendary, and Burns gave Forest four seasons-worth of top-class service, winning umpteen medals and plaudits before leaving for Leeds United in 1981 for £400,000 as the championship-winning side began to break up. He moved to Derby County in 1984, then had brief spells with Notts County, Barnsley and Swedish side Elfsborg before moving into non-league football.

THE ONLY FOREST MAN TO WIN THE SPORTSWRITERS' PLAYER OF THE SEASON AWARD, KENNY BURNS, JOINED THE CLUB ON THE 17TH JULY 1977

THURSDAY 18th JULY 1991

Brian Clough paid out the final big transfer fee of his Forest career, signing Millwall's Teddy Sheringham for £2 million. Sheringham had finished the previous season as the league's top scorer, with 33 goals in 46 Second Division games. He would make the step up with a degree of success with the Reds (14 goals in 42 games) before moving on to loftier heights with Tottenham Hotspur, Manchester United and England.

FRIDAY 19th JULY 1974

26-goal striker Duncan McKenzie was placed on the transfer list after contract negotiations broke down, meaning the £250,000-rated player was likely to have played his last game in a Forest shirt.

MONDAY 19th JULY 1993

The Reds set a new British transfer fee record by selling star 21-year-old midfielder Roy Keane to Manchester United for £3.75 million. Following Forest's relegation Keane's departure seemed somewhat inevitable, despite the player agreeing a lucrative new contract with Forest, the terms of which had caused Brian Clough to label the young Irishman 'a greedy child'. That contract contained a relegation clause which Keane activated and he agreed a £4 million move to Blackburn Rovers, ending speculation that he was about to join Arsenal. One day before the deal became official, United boss Alex Ferguson rang Keane and asked him if he would consider a move to Old Trafford instead. Keane agreed and cancelled his agreement with Blackburn, much to the chagrin of Blackburn boss Kenny Dalglish. Keane replaced 36-year-old Bryan Robson in United's midfield and, just as he did when he unexpectedly broke into Forest's first team, never looked back.

FRIDAY 20th JULY 1979

Forest replaced the retired Frank Clark and the injured Colin Barrett by splashing out half a million pounds on Leeds United left-back Frank Gray. Gray was a quietly effective player and almost ever-present during two years with Forest before returning to Leeds in the summer of 1981 for £400,000. He won a European Cup winners' medal with Forest in 1980.

TUESDAY 21st JULY 2009

Defender Joel Lynch became the latest ex-loanee, joining Chris Gunter, Dexter Blackstock and Lee Camp, to join Forest in a permanent deal, costing the club £200,000. The Brighton & Hove Albion player had spent a few weeks at Forest at the tail end of the 2008/09 season, providing back-up for the club's defensive positions.

THURSDAY 22nd JULY 1999

David Platt began his enjoyment of Nigel Doughty's wallet by spending £3 million on Aston Villa utility man Riccardo Scimeca. Scimeca had been on Villa's books since 1995 and, despite starting 50 games, never managed to successfully hold down a regular place, so eyebrows were raised at Forest's spend on a top-flight squad player. Scimeca took time to settle at the club – he was used in a number of positions, but usually occupied central defence or midfield. He had his best spell in the 2002/03 season, settling into a defensive midfield spot and helping the club into the play-offs. This was Forest's make-or-break season and their eventual failure to Sheffield United meant the high-earning Scimeca joined a few fellow team-mates in leaving the club, joining Leicester City on a free in June 2003. He later went on to play for West Bromwich Albion and Cardiff City before injury forced his retirement in May 2010.

MONDAY 23rd JULY 1959

Billy Walker used some of the funds generated by Forest's successful FA Cup run to acquire midfielder Jim Iley from Tottenham Hotspur for a club record fee. Iley would add a touch of class to Forest's play for three seasons with a century of appearances until he signed for Joe Harvey's Newcastle United to aid their promotion charge from the old Second Division, something they eventually achieved in 1964/65. Jim would give his best years to the Magpies before leaving for Peterborough United during the 1968/69 season.

THURSDAY 23rd JULY 1984

Right-back Viv Anderson called time on his decade-long Forest career by signing for Arsenal in a £250,000 deal. The tremendously popular defender would go on to represent Manchester United, Sheffield Wednesday, Barnsley and Middlesbrough.

WEDNESDAY 24th JULY 1991

Defender Des Walker was reportedly the subject of a £4.4 million bid from Real Madrid, which Forest turned down.

MONDAY 24th JULY 1995

Possibly the worst transfer deal in Forest's history (certainly one to rival the £100,000 purchase of Jim Baxter and the £1 million paid for Justin Fashanu) was completed, as Frank Clark decided it was perfectly legitimate to throw £1.8 million at Torino for Italian striker Andrea Silenzi. Tall and gangly, Silenzi appeared ill-at-ease on the football field, and barely played at all for Forest, managing 12 league appearances in two years and no goals (although he did manage two goals in cups against the might of Bradford City and Oxford United). How he won a cap for Italy is anyone's guess – as pundit Alan Hansen put it, 'if this guy played for Italy, they must have had a major flu epidemic amongst all their other forwards at the time'. Silenzi was eventually sent on loan to Venezia, and when told to return by Dave Bassett, refused. Bassett tore up the Italian's contract there and then.

FRIDAY 25th JULY 1980

Forest were in America as part of a three-game tour, taking on the Tampa Bay Rowdies. Despite being the current European champions the Reds were held to a 0-0 draw. Forest were restricted to just three shots on target all game, with Garry Birtles finding himself thwarted by Tampa Bay goalie Winston DuBose in the game's best chance. Forest also drew 1-1 with Vancouver Whitecaps and beat Toronto Blizzard 3-1 while in North America.

MONDAY 26th JULY 2010

The Reds took on Claude Puel's Champions League semi-finalists Olympique Lyonnais (who beat Spanish giants Real Madrid on the way to that semi-final) in a pre-season friendly at the City Ground. A decent crowd of 7,178 watched Forest lose 3-1, with the French side's goals coming from €13 million man Baferimbi Gomis (2) and Jimmy Briand (a bargain at €6 million). Dele Adebola (a free transfer) scored for the home side, converting Nathan Tyson's mis-hit effort.

FRIDAY 27th JULY 1984

A busy day for the Reds and their chequebook as they completed a trio of signings, namely giant Dutchman Johnny Metgod from Real Madrid, midfielder Gary Megson from Sheffield Wednesday, and winger Franz Carr from Blackburn Rovers. The three players would cost a total of £400,000, although in the case of Metgod and Carr (who cost only £25,000) it would prove money well spent.

SATURDAY 28th JULY 2001

A groundbreaking tie for Forest as they took on India's national side in a friendly at the City Ground, coming out 2-0 victors. Having lost 3-0 to Brentford on Tuesday, India seemed determined to put on a better show, but despite their reportedly improved performance they still went behind to Eugen Bopp's firm strike on 18. A quarter of an hour later Jack Lester doubled Forest's advantage with a penalty. The Reds were frustrated for the rest of the match and Jules Alberto came close to pulling one back for India, forcing an excellent save from Darren Ward. India would conclude their tour with a draw with Leyton Orient and a loss to Walsall.

TUESDAY 29th JULY 1986

On a tour of Sweden Forest beat Aelmhult 8-0, with Neil Webb scoring six goals. The other scorers were Colin Walsh and T Ringberg, who was the tour courier and was allowed to come on as a substitute for the final ten minutes of the game.

SUNDAY 30th JULY 2001

With debts standing at £6 million and weekly losses of £100,000, newly-installed manager Paul Hart was summoned to a meeting with the club's hierarchy and told that Forest's financial situation would force the club to listen to any offer made for one of his first-team players.

FRIDAY 31st JULY 1987

Nigel Clough scored four goals in a friendly at Swedish club Waggeryds IK. The other scorers were David Campbell (2) and Brian Rice.

NOTTINGHAM FOREST
On This Day

AUGUST

THURSDAY 1st AUGUST 1974

Goalkeeper Jim Barron ended his association with Forest by signing for Swindon Town on a free transfer. The ex-Chelsea keeper had been signed from Oxford United in 1970 as a replacement for Alan Hill and had been Forest's regular custodian ever since, providing steady if unspectacular service, but the emergence of Denis Peacock, Peter Wells and John Middleton meant his days were numbered.

WEDNESDAY 1st AUGUST 1979

A full-strength Forest were trounced 5-0 by Bayern Munich in the Olympic Stadium. Their previous game there? The small matter of victory in the European Cup final against Malmo, two months previously.

TUESDAY 2nd AUGUST 1966

The first-ever Icelander to play for Forest, Thorvaldur 'Toddy' Orlygsson, was born in Akureyri. Signed for an Icelandic record of £175,000 from KA Akureyri, Brian Clough described him as the best signing he had ever made, but, after an initially exciting debut at home to Southampton on December 17th 1989, Orlygsson's confidence seemed to evaporate and he faded completely from the first-team picture. He made a few more appearances after a year's break and looked more of the player his reputation had predicted, but never firmly established himself at the club. He went on to play for Stoke and Oldham before returning to KA Akureyri in 1999.

SUNDAY 3rd AUGUST 1975

Forest enjoyed a day of goals in a pre-season match on tour in West Germany when they beat TSV Gaimersheim 9-0. The scorers were George Lyall (2), John O'Hare (2), Barry Butlin (2), Tony Woodcock (2) and Jimmy McIntosh.

TUESDAY 3rd AUGUST 1982

Brian Clough signed a familiar face in recruiting former England international and Derby County defender Colin Todd from Birmingham City, replacing the recent loss of Kenny Burns and David Needham. Injuries thwarted Todd's time at Forest, and he left for Oxford United in 1984.

TUESDAY 4th AUGUST 1998

Ominously, Pierre van Hooijdonk failed to turn up for the start of pre-season training in preparation for the 1998/99 season. The giant Dutchman claimed that it was Forest's perceived lack of ambition that led him to putting in a transfer request, then he refused to return to England when it was not granted. Forest's players had other ideas, though. 'Pierre has tried to hold the club to ransom,' said goalkeeper Mark Crossley. 'It is blackmail. Basically, one of our players has gone on strike and left the others to get on with the job.'

TUESDAY 5th AUGUST 1986

There was more goalscoring fun for Forest in pre-season friendlies with a one-sided 12-0 defeat of MSC Meppel in the Netherlands. Leading the scoring was young striker Phil Starbuck, who helped himself to five goals. Brian Rice scored a hat-trick, Mark Smalley scored twice, Franz Carr once and there was one own goal.

TUESDAY 6th AUGUST 1974

The current 'most wanted youngster in football', Forest's 26-goal striker Duncan McKenzie, finally sealed a £240,000 deal to join Brian Clough's Leeds United.

SATURDAY 6th AUGUST 1977

Forest's longest-serving player, uncomplicated defender Robert 'Sammy' Chapman, joined Notts County on a free transfer, ending a 15-year association with the Reds. Chapman had begun with the Reds as an inside-forward, then as a half-back before settling into a role as a centre-half who seldom took prisoners. He would play one ever-present season with County before moving on to Shrewsbury Town and then Burton Albion to finish off his career.

MONDAY 6th AUGUST 1979

In what turned out to be one of the poorest decisions of his managerial career, Brian Clough allowed Archie Gemmill to leave the club for Birmingham City. Gemmill reportedly remained sore about sitting out the 1979 European Cup final. Clough spent the next three years trying to replace his lost midfield engine.

TUESDAY 6th AUGUST 1985

In a surprising move, John Robertson rejoined Forest after two uninspiring seasons with Derby County. Robertson began 1985/86 in his familiar number 11 shirt, but it soon became clear much of the old magic had gone, and 11 games later his City Ground career was finally over – this time for good.

SATURDAY 7th AUGUST 1982

Forest continued their pre-season tour after a 3-0 win over a Malaysia Select XI with a 3-1 defeat to Athletic Bilbao in Spain in which Justin Fashanu and John Robertson were sent off.

SATURDAY 7th AUGUST 1999

The 1999/2000 season kicked off early because of the 2000 European Championships, meaning an extra-early start to the managerial career at Forest of David Platt. Salvatore Matrecano, Moreno Mannini, Gianluca Petrachi and Ricky Scimeca all made their debuts in a game against Ipswich at Portman Road, but to very little avail as goals by Richard Naylor, David Johnson (whom Platt would eventually splash £3 million on) and Jamie Scowcroft condemned Platt's new side to a 3-1 defeat. Forest's goal came from a penalty by Chris Bart-Williams, given when Marlon Harewood was tripped in the box by Manuel Thetis…

SATURDAY 8th AUGUST 1979

…while 20 years previously, in another early-start season due to the European Championships, Forest started out at Portman Road again, this time successfully with a 1-0 win. Tony Woodcock scored the only goal of the game a minute after the break, and there'd been debuts for summer signings Frank Gray and Asa Hartford.

THURSDAY 8th AUGUST 1985

The Reds signed 21-year-old Scottish midfielder Brian Rice from Hibernian. Rice would spend six years at the City Ground, mainly on the left wing. He would become a cult figure, inspiring the song based on the Beatles' 'Yellow Submarine' – 'Number one, is Brian Rice. Number two, is Brian Rice. Number three, is Brian Rice…'

SATURDAY 8th AUGUST 1987

Forest's Neil Webb played for the Football League XI against the Rest of the World XI at Wembley in the English Football League Centenary Classic, a match held in celebration of 100 years of the Football League. In a match noted for the continual booing of the Rest of the World XI's Diego Maradona, the League side won 3-0, with all the goals coming from Manchester United players – two from Bryan Robson and one from Norman Whiteside.

SATURDAY 9th AUGUST 2003

Mick McCarthy brought his Sunderland side to the City Ground following their relegation the previous term from the Premiership, fresh on the back of 15 straight league defeats. They added one to that list, going down 2-0 through first-half strikes by Marlon Harewood and Matthieu Louis-Jean.

FRIDAY 10th AUGUST 1979

Following their unbelievable win over Malmo in May, there was more European success for the Reds with victory in the slightly less prestigious Bilbao Tournament in Spain. They beat Dynamo Bucharest in the final 2-1, with two goals (one a penalty) from John Robertson.

WEDNESDAY 10th AUGUST 1988

Former Reds midfielder Steve Hodge returned to the City Ground in a £550,000 move from Tottenham Hotspur. A local lad, Hodge had joined Forest for his first spell in 1980 as an apprentice, making his debut against Ipswich Town in the final game of the 1981/82 season. 'Harry' Hodge immediately became an important member of Forest's midfield before a need to balance the books saw him sold to Aston Villa two games into the 1985/86 season. England recognition followed and he moved on to Tottenham in November 1986. He played in the 1986 World Cup finals and was the man whose backpass/sliced clearance was headed home by Diego Maradona's 'Hand of God'. Back with Forest, Hodge soon rediscovered both his form and England career. He was sold again, this time to Leeds United for an inflated £900,000 in the summer of 1991.

SATURDAY 10th AUGUST 2002

Des Walker made a second debut for Nottingham Forest, more than 18 years after his first. Walker had first come to prominence with the Reds in the mid-to-late 1980s as a virtually unbeatable defender with pace and impeccable timing and, after an inspiring time at Italia '90, came to be regarded as one of Europe's finest defenders. A move to Sampdoria followed, which, mainly due to injury and being played at left-back, didn't work out. He returned to England in 1993 with Sheffield Wednesday, serving the Owls almost as well as he had served Forest before leaving in 2001. After a very brief stint with Burton Albion, then-Forest boss Paul Hart invited Walker to train with the Reds in the summer of 2002, and the veteran surprised everyone by impressing enough to be handed a contract. He would play a further 60 games for Forest, forming an excellent defensive partnership with the fledgling Michael Dawson, until finally retiring in 2004. He moved onto Forest's coaching staff but left in January 2005 when Gary Megson was appointed.

MONDAY 11th AUGUST 1997

Forest scored eight goals in a game for the first time in almost half a century, slamming Doncaster Rovers 8-0 in the first round of the Coca-Cola Cup. The goals came from Geoff Thomas, Dean Saunders (2), Jon Olav Hjelde (2), Pierre van Hooijdonk (2) and Chris Allen.

SATURDAY 12th AUGUST 1978

Football League champions Nottingham Forest hammered FA Cup winners Ipswich Town 5-0 in the 1978 FA Charity Shield. Ipswich were missing their defensive pairing of Kevin Beattie and Allan Hunter, and could not find any way past Peter Shilton despite having the better of the first half. Forest's goals came from Martin O'Neill (2), Peter Withe (his last goal for the club), Larry Lloyd and John Robertson.

TUESDAY 12th AUGUST 1981

Mark Proctor was snapped up for £425,000 from Middlesbrough. Rated as a significant prospect, it wouldn't work out for him at the City Ground and he was sold to Sunderland in 1983.

TUESDAY 13th AUGUST 1974

Allan Brown began to spend the money garnered by Duncan McKenzie's sale to Leeds United by buying AFC Bournemouth's promising Welsh defender David Jones. At home at left-back or centre-back, Jones would only survive one season at the City Ground before being sold to Norwich City.

SATURDAY 14th AUGUST 1971

Forest opened up the 1971/72 campaign with a 3-1 defeat at Liverpool, an Ian Storey-Moore penalty the only response to goals by Kevin Keegan, Tommy Smith (penalty) and Emlyn Hughes. Things would seldom improve for the rest of a season which culminated in relegation.

SATURDAY 15th AUGUST 1959

The Reds made their first ever appearance in the FA Charity Shield following their FA Cup final win against Luton Town the previous May, but were defeated 3-1 by champions Wolverhampton Wanderers at Molineux. Peter Broadbent, Mickey Lill and Jimmy Murray scored the goals for Wolves, with Tommy Wilson replying.

SATURDAY 15th AUGUST 1970

A win over Coventry City was how Forest began the 1970/71 season, with goals by Barry Lyons and Ian Storey-Moore, and debuts for goalkeeper Jim Barron and attacking midfielder Peter Cormack.

SATURDAY 16th AUGUST 1969

Don Revie brought his all-conquering Leeds United side to the City Ground with the men in white having gone 30 games without defeat, equalling a top-flight record set by Burnley in 1921. In a niggly game, the score was deadlocked until the 68th minute, when Allan Clarke scored his 100th league goal, and then further strikes from Peter Lorimer, Eddie Gray and Johnny Giles sealed an impressive 4-1 victory, with Ronnie Rees replying for Forest. The game was briefly enlivened by the appearance of a Great Dane on the pitch, holding up play for a few minutes before being ushered off. Leeds would go four more games before being beaten 3-2 by Everton at Goodison Park.

SATURDAY 16th AUGUST 1975

During a league game with Plymouth at the City Ground, invading Argyle fans met an unexpected deterrent in Forest boss Brian Clough, who rose from the dugout and ordered them back into the stands.

SATURDAY 17th AUGUST 1985

Forest were the first visitors to Luton Town's notorious plastic pitch. New signing Neil Webb made a goalscoring debut as he equalised Brian Stein's opener to give Forest a 1-1 draw.

SATURDAY 17th AUGUST 1996

Kevin Campbell, who'd spent most of his first year at Forest either injured or lacking form, began the new 1996/97 season with a hat-trick within 47 minutes at Highfield Road as Forest bashed Coventry City 3-0. Alas, this would prove to be something of a false dawn for man and club, as Campbell would only score another three goals all season, and Forest ended up bottom of the Premiership.

SATURDAY 17th AUGUST 1991

The Reds opened up the 1991/92 season parading almost £3.5 million of new talent in Carl Tiler and Teddy Sheringham. They beat Everton 2-1 at the City Ground, Nigels Clough and Jemson scoring for Forest, with a Stuart Pearce own goal for the Toffeemen.

SATURDAY 18th AUGUST 1956

Stewart Imlach made his debut for Forest in 4-1 victory at Leyton Orient after signing from Derby County for £5,000. He would remain on Forest's left wing for four seasons, providing ample crosses for the likes of Tommy Wilson, before losing his place in the side and being sold to Luton Town for £8,000 in 1960. Short spells with Coventry City and Crystal Palace would follow before he moved successfully into coaching with Notts County, Everton, Blackpool and Bury. Stewart would become the subject of a popular football book, *My Father and Other Working Class Football Heroes*, written by his journalist son, Gary. Stewart passed away in Lossiemouth in 2001.

SATURDAY 19th AUGUST 1978

Forest started the defence of their title at home, but were forced to play second fiddle to a freshly-promoted Tottenham Hotspur side containing the surprise additions of the summer transfer market, Argentinians Ricardo Villa and Osvaldo Ardiles. Forest drew the opening fixture 1-1, with Martin O'Neill's opener cancelled out by Villa on his debut.

SATURDAY 19th AUGUST 1995

Matthew Le Tissier scored a hat-trick (two penalties) in the opening game of the 1995/96 season for Southampton against Forest at The Dell. He found himself on the losing side, though, as goals by Colin Cooper, Ian Woan and two from Bryan Roy saw Forest win by the odd goal in seven.

SATURDAY 20th AUGUST 1949

Wally Ardron made a scoring debut after his recruitment from Rotherham United in a 2-2 draw at Brighton & Hove Albion. The other goal came from Brighton wing-half Jess Willard.

SATURDAY 20th AUGUST 1977

Forest were back in the top flight after a five-year absence and celebrated with an unexpected 3-1 victory at Everton. Peter Withe and John Robertson gave Forest a 2-0 lead before Jim Pearson pulled one back for Gordon Lee's side a minute before half-time. Martin O'Neill sealed the win about ten minutes before the end.

THURSDAY 20th AUGUST 1981

One of the longest player chases finally dragged to a conclusion when Justin Fashanu finally signed from Norwich City for £1 million, becoming Britain's first black footballer to move for the landmark fee. The football marriage of the gay former Barnado's boy and the brash northerner Brian Clough could hardly have been a worse match, and Fashanu's confidence swiftly evaporated. He would score a mere four goals in 36 games before moving to Notts County in December 1982 for £150,000. From that point on Fashanu would play for countless clubs, and his sexuality and lifestyle generated yards of column inches.

THURSDAY 20th AUGUST 1998

Forest's support suffered a real shock when it was announced that popular club skipper Colin Cooper was to be sold to Middlesbrough for £2.5 million – due, it was claimed, to a 'gentlemen's agreement' between Cooper and Forest boss Dave Bassett, who'd agreed to allow Cooper to rejoin his first club should they ever come in for him. On the same day, Bassett snapped up promising Queens Park Rangers midfielder Nigel Quashie for the same fee.

MONDAY 21st AUGUST 1978

A hugely surprising transfer move as Peter Withe went to Newcastle United for £200,000, having only made one appearance in the 1978/79 season. The much-travelled striker had joined Forest from Birmingham City for £45,000 and worn the number nine shirt, providing a perfect partner for Tony Woodcock and a goalscoring end to much of John Robertson's best work. Withe would spend two seasons at St James' Park before moving to Aston Villa for £500,000, where he'd play the best football of his career, winning the league, European Cup and 11 England caps.

WEDNESDAY 21st AUGUST 1991

The irony was lost on no one as Stuart Pearce collected the PFA Fair Play award for Forest and was then sent off for swearing during a 3-1 defeat to Tottenham Hotspur at the City Ground. On the same day, Brian Clough said he would resign if Nottingham City Council's proposed ground share scheme with Notts County was given the green light.

SATURDAY 22nd AUGUST 1992

In what turned out to be Teddy Sheringham's final game for Forest, the Reds were slaughtered 5-3 by Oldham Athletic at Boundary Park, with the Latics 5-0 up after an hour. A tardy salvage attempt by Stuart Pearce and Gary Bannister (2) was too late.

THURSDAY 23rd AUGUST 1979

Brian Clough stopped Trevor Francis' wages when the million-pound man returned from Detroit Express with a groin strain.

JUSTIN FASHANU, THE FIRST BLACK PLAYER IN ENGLAND TO COMMAND A £1M FEE, BEGAN HIS FOREST NIGHTMARE ON 20TH AUGUST 1981

SATURDAY 24th AUGUST 1968

A tragic day for Forest as a fire broke out in the dressing room area of the main stand during a league game against Leeds United, swiftly spreading and consuming the entire stand. Fortunately – and miraculously – there were no casualties amongst the 31,126 crowd. Many of the club's records, trophies and items of memorabilia were lost in the fire. The game was abandoned and Forest were forced to play their next six 'home' league games at Notts County's Meadow Lane, winning none of them.

SATURDAY 25th AUGUST 1956

Jim Barrett continued his goalscoring start to the season with a hat-trick against Fulham in the first City Ground game of the season, which finished 3-1 to Forest. This followed his doubles at Leyton Orient (4-1) and Bristol City (5-1), meaning he'd scored seven in his first three games. Barrett would end the season with 30 from 37 games.

THURSDAY 26th AUGUST 1982

Brian Clough finally replaced Peter Shilton by recruiting the excellent Dutch international goalkeeper Hans van Breukelen from FC Utrecht for £200,000. Van Breukelen would be an immense presence in the Forest goal for two seasons before returning home and to PSV Eindhoven, whom he'd go on to serve for a decade.

SATURDAY 27th AUGUST 2005

Forest beat Gillingham 3-1 at Priestfield Stadium with goals by David Johnson, Scott Dobie and Spencer Weir-Daley. They would not win away from home again until February 18th 2006, which coincidentally (or not) would be Frank Barlow and Charlie McParland's first game in charge following the end of Gary Megson's managerial reign.

THURSDAY 28th AUGUST 1975

Terry Curran was signed from Doncaster Rovers for £60,000 plus reserve team winger Ian Miller. Curran would terrorise opposition full-backs until an injury in October 1976 sidelined him, and he never managed to win his place back from Martin O'Neill.

FRIDAY 28th AUGUST 1992

Forest's best player of 1991/92, Teddy Sheringham, was sold to Tottenham Hotspur for £2.1 million. Brian Clough would replace Sheringham with veteran Gary Bannister and the unprolific Robert Rosario, resulting in relegation at the end of the season.

WEDNESDAY 29th AUGUST 1979

While his team-mates drew 1-1 at Blackburn Rovers in the League Cup, Forest midfielder Asa Hartford had more personal matters to attend to, finalising a transfer to Everton after a mere three appearances for the Reds.

SATURDAY 30th AUGUST 1919

Football restarted after the enforced break due to the First World War. Forest lost 2-0 in a Second Division fixture at Rotherham County with no less than six players making their debuts for the club: Billy Shearman, Fred Parker, Jack Lythgoe, Joe Mills, Harry Bulling and Joe Johnson.

FRIDAY 30th AUGUST 1991

The Reds finally completed their £4.5 million chequebook flourishing with the signing of winger Kingsley Black from Luton Town. The young Irishman joined fellow big-money buys Teddy Sheringham and Carl Tiler at the City Ground.

TUESDAY 30th AUGUST 1994

Forest drew 1-1 at home to Manchester United (Stan Collymore replying to an Andrei Kanchelskis goal) and suddenly and unexpectedly found themselves on top of the Premiership table.

SATURDAY 31st AUGUST 1946

The Reds journeyed to Barnsley for the start of the 1946/47 season, their first league match since September 1939, when competition was suspended due to the outbreak of World War II. They lost 3-2, with George Robledo scoring a hat-trick for Barnsley. Forest's goalscorers were 'Sailor' Brown and Frank O'Donnell. Both these players were making their debuts for the club, as was forward Tom Hinchcliffe in his only appearance for the Reds.

NOTTINGHAM FOREST
On This Day

SEPTEMBER

SATURDAY 1st SEPTEMBER 1984

Forest's Peter Davenport scored the first top-flight hat-trick of the season against Sunderland at the City Ground. His goals came in the 13th, 52nd and 62nd minutes, with Colin West scoring one for the Rokerites after 17 minutes.

TUESDAY 1st SEPTEMBER 1992

Graham Taylor announced that Forest skipper Stuart Pearce was to be the new captain of England in succession to the recently retired Gary Lineker.

SATURDAY 2nd SEPTEMBER 1893

Nottingham Forest commenced their second season in the Football League with a handsome 7-1 victory over Wolverhampton Wanderers. Debutant James Collins, who had recently left Newcastle United, scored four times, with the other goals coming from Arthur Shaw and Neil McCallum (2).

WEDNESDAY 2nd SEPTEMBER 1981

The fractious relationship between Trevor Francis and Brian Clough finally came to an end when Britain's first million-pound footballer was sold to Manchester City for £1.2 million. Francis would only play 26 games at Maine Road before moving into Italian football with Sampdoria and then Atalanta. He returned to Britain with Glasgow Rangers in 1987 and then played out his career with Queens Park Rangers and Sheffield Wednesday.

SATURDAY 3rd SEPTEMBER 1892

Forest, newly elected straight into Division One of the expanded Football League as the 1892/93 Football Alliance champions, opened their initial Football League campaign with a 2-2 draw at Goodison Park against Everton (also the first ever league game at Everton's new ground following their move from Anfield). 'Sandy' Higgins and Horace Pike were Forest's scorers. Forest: Brown, Earp, Scott, Hamilton, Albert Smith, McCracken, McCallum, 'Tich' Smith, Higgins, Pike, McInnes. Left-winger Tom McInnes was making his Forest debut, the Glaswegian having signed recently from Clyde.

SATURDAY 3rd SEPTEMBER 1898

The Reds played their first game at the new City Ground, after moving from the Town Ground. Their opponents were Blackburn Rovers, who spoilt the party somewhat by winning 1-0.

SATURDAY 4th SEPTEMBER 1897

Alf Spouncer made his debut from Forest in the league in a 1-1 draw at the Town Ground against Notts County. Born in Gainsborough on 1st July 1877, Alf joined Forest from Gainsborough Trinity after a brief spell with Sheffield United and settled into the left-wing berth, forcing Tom McInnes to move to the right. He won an FA Cup winners' medal in 1898 and one cap for England against Wales in 1900. Spouncer served Forest for a dozen years until retiring in 1910, later coaching in Europe including a spell at Barcelona. He went on to work in the flour trade and served in the Black Watch during the First World War. Forest lost the last surviving member of the 1898 FA Cup final winning side when Alf passed away on 31st August 1962.

MONDAY 4th SEPTEMBER 1965

Barry McArthur became Forest's first ever used substitute following the introduction of a number 12 at the start of the season. He came on for Chris Crowe at Leeds United in a 2-1 defeat. It was also McArthur's league debut.

TUESDAY 5th SEPTEMBER 1967

A 51st minute goal from Emlyn Hughes gave Liverpool a 1-0 victory at the City Ground to end Forest's sequence of 28 unbeaten home games. The last team to beat Forest at home had been Stoke City, who'd won 2-1 in the first game of the 1966/67 season.

WEDNESDAY 5th SEPTEMBER 1984

Forest recorded their highest-ever win at Villa Park, beating the Villans 5-0. New striker Trevor Christie aped his strike partner, Peter Davenport, by scoring a hat-trick – as 'Dav' had done in the previous game against Sunderland. The other Forest scorers were Ian Bowyer and Steve Hodge.

WEDNESDAY 6th SEPTEMBER 2000

Another mark was set to display the depths to which the former European champions had sunk as Forest were dumped out of the Worthington Cup by Darlington. Having drawn the first leg at Feethams 2-2 Forest must have been confident of progressing to the next round but it was not to be, despite Stern John giving them the lead on nine minutes. Late goals by Paul Campbell and Shaun Elliott handed the tie to the Quakers.

WEDNESDAY 7th SEPTEMBER 1977

In the *Daily Mirror*, ex-Leeds United custodian Gary Sprake made claims that Don Revie, the Leeds manager during their all-conquering days of the late 1960s and early 1970s, had once attempted to bribe Forest goalkeeper Jim Barron. Barron himself revealed that once Billy Bremner was sent into the Forest dressing room by Revie with a request for the Reds to 'go easy' – a request that was vehemently rejected.

SATURDAY 7th SEPTEMBER 1996

Steve Stone suffered a ruptured knee tendon in a 0-0 home draw against Leicester City which saw him miss the rest of the season. The energetic midfielder's season-long absence was a crucial factor in Forest's relegation from the top flight that term.

WEDNESDAY 8th SEPTEMBER 2010

Never one it seemed to shy away from letting the media know how he felt, Forest manager Billy Davies allegedly made a 'back me or sack me' ultimatum in the *Daily Mirror* to Forest's board. Davies' displeasure at the lack of signings at the end of the 2009/10 term and during the close season had already been well heard. For once, Davies' bleatings must have been listened to as Marcus Tudgay, Robbie Findlay, Paul Konchesky, Aaron Ramsey and Kris Boyd were all signed in the forthcoming months.

SATURDAY 9th SEPTEMBER 1978

Gary Mills made his debut for Forest at home in a 2-1 victory over Arsenal and, at 16 years and 302 days, became the youngest player ever to represent the Reds in the league.

SATURDAY 9th SEPTEMBER 1995

Andrea Silenzi finally became the first Italian to play in the Premiership, making his debut as a 52nd minute substitute for Kevin Campbell in a 1-1 draw at Coventry City. Cheered onto the pitch by the visiting Forest fans, Stuart Pearce floated a long ball over to the gangly striker, who mistimed his header and fell flat on his face. This turned out to be one of the highlights of Silenzi's career in a red shirt.

SATURDAY 10th SEPTEMBER 1960

Andy Beattie handed a surprise debut to Richard 'Flip' Le Flem who, at 18 years and 31 days, became Forest's youngest-ever league player. A pacy and skilful winger, the Guernsey-born Flip was the latest Channel Islander to be recommended to the club by scout Ted Malpass, a former team-mate of ex-Forest boss Billy Walker at Aston Villa, following the likes of Bill Whare and Geoff Vowden. He would remain on the left wing for Forest until he was swapped for Wolverhampton Wanderers' Alan Hinton in 1964, later playing for Middlesbrough and Leyton Orient. He scored one of the best ever goals for the club, against Burnley in 1962 (see December 1st).

SATURDAY 10th SEPTEMBER 1977

John Middleton made his final appearance for Forest in a 3-2 defeat of Wolverhampton Wanderers at Molinuex. The young keeper, an England Under-21 international thought to be bound for full international honours, was criticised after this match by Brian Clough for conceding five goals in his last two games, and steps were hence made to speed up the acquisition of Peter Shilton. Middleton would form part of the exchange deal, along with £25,000, which brought Archie Gemmill to the City Ground later that month. It would never work out for Middleton at the Baseball Ground and injury forced his premature retirement in 1980.

MONDAY 11th SEPTEMBER 1961

A double first for Forest as they entered the Football League Cup for the first time and also played under floodlights, against Gillingham at the City Ground. Forest won 4-1, with goals from Geoff Vowden (2), Colin Booth and Colin Addison.

SATURDAY 12th SEPTEMBER 1981

The combative Forest midfielder David Prutton was born in Hull. One of the first products of Forest's successful youth policy at the turn of the century (along with Jermaine Jenas, Michael Dawson and Andy Reid), Prutton was given his chance a few weeks into the 1999/00 season and never looked back, providing a string of mature performances that belied his tender age while other (older and more experienced) players floundered. The club's financial perils saw him sold to Southampton for £2.5 million in March 2003, where he eventually struggled after a promising start. He returned to Forest on loan at the end of the 2006/07 season, but let the club down when he was sent off in the 90th minute of the second leg of the play-off against Yeovil, leaving the team to play extra time with ten men. He later joined Leeds United, Colchester United and Swindon Town.

WEDNESDAY 13th SEPTEMBER 1961

Forest played in official European competition for the first time, travelling to Spain to take on giants Valencia in the Inter-Cities Fairs Cup, their qualification based on the city's annual Goose Fair. Forest battled throughout in front of 46,000 supporters, but two goals from Brazilian Waldo were enough to secure a 2-0 victory for 'Los Che'.

TUESDAY 13th SEPTEMBER 1977

Brian Clough and Peter Taylor secured a massive piece in their Forest championship squad building project by splashing a club record £240,000 on England goalkeeper Peter Shilton. The former Leicester City custodian had impressed so much as a youngster with the Foxes that the club allowed the legendary Gordon Banks to join Stoke, and Shilton also replaced Banks at Stoke, but a downturn in his fortunes saw City slide out of the top flight and Liverpool's Ray Clemence take the yellow international jersey as England's number one. Shilton would settle straight between Forest's goalposts and with the supreme defensive duo Larry Lloyd and Kenny Burns ahead of him would go on to concede a mere 18 goals in the remaining 37 league games of the season. He went on to regain a place in the England team (although he had to alternate goalkeeping duties with Clemence) and win the PFA Player of the Season award.

WEDNESDAY 13th SEPTEMBER 1978

One of the best Forest nights of European football, albeit against familiar opposition in Liverpool. Drawn in the European Cup against their fiercest rivals, Forest were very much second favourites entering the tie, having made a poor start to the season and sold Peter Withe. Liverpool, by contrast, had started 1978/79 with five straight wins. Brian Clough sprung one of his usual surprises by keeping faith with the untried Garry Birtles as Withe's replacement for only the youngster's third first-team outing. Just before the half-hour a typical flowing Forest move involving Ian Bowyer and Tony Woodcock ended up with Birtles having a simple chance to score his first senior goal, which he held his nerve to take. The game progressed with very few chances for either side, but Liverpool made a capital mistake in settling for a 1-0 defeat which they were obviously confident of overturning at Anfield. Two minutes from the end they were left rueing their decision as Birtles crossed the ball, Woodcock nodded it down and left-back Colin Barrett, inexplicably finding himself in the penalty area, volleyed home a rocket that Liverpool keeper Ray Clemence only saw once it had burst into the back of the net.

SATURDAY 13th SEPTEMBER 1986

Forest hit top spot with a decisive 6-0 win over Aston Villa, for whom only Tony Daley seemed to have any appetite to play football. The scorers for Forest were Franz Carr, Garry Birtles (2), Nigel Clough and Neil Webb (2). Villa boss Graham Turner's Sunday lunch was ruined the following day by the news that he was out of a job.

SATURDAY 14th SEPTEMBER 1963

Calvin Palmer played his final game for Nottingham Forest in a 1-0 victory for the Reds at Stoke City. The Skegness-born half-back had broken into the first team in 1960 as a youngster and initially as a striker before reverting to the back line and ousting Jeff Whitefoot from the team. He was thought to be odds-on for a glittering career and became one of the club's youngest-ever captains but injuries, a loss of form and the emergence of Henry Newton saw him fall from favour. He was sold to Stoke City in 1963, moving on to Sunderland after four virtually ever-present seasons in the Potteries.

MONDAY 14th SEPTEMBER 1970

Forest took part in the inaugural 'British Isles Cup' or, officially, the 'International League Board Competition' – later rebranded as the 'Texaco Cup' once sponsorship had been secured for the invitation competition for English, Scottish and Irish teams. They hosted Airdrieonians in the first leg at the City Ground, drawing 2-2 with goals from Peter Cormack and Ian Storey-Moore. Two weeks later they travelled to Airdrie for the second leg, again drawing 2-2. Both goals were scored, appropriately, by Scots – Dave Hilley and Cormack again. After extra time penalty kicks were used to separate the sides, Forest losing the shoot-out 5-4. Airdrie would be knocked out in the second round by Hearts, who would then lose the final to Wolverhampton Wanderers.

SATURDAY 15th SEPTEMBER 1956

The legendary right-winger Freddie Scott played his last game for Forest in a 3-2 defeat against Rotherham United. His appearance, less than a month before his 40th birthday, made him Forest's oldest ever outfield player (Forest's oldest ever player is goalkeeper Dave Beasant, who played for the Reds at the age of 42). The diminutive winger had signed for Forest from York City a decade previously, having played for Bradford City and Bolton Wanderers. Scott would have been right at home in any of Brian Clough's sides, being a lover of the ball and the deliverer of a constant supply of fine crosses, many of them primed to encounter Wally Ardron's forehead. He was first choice for seven of his ten years at the club until injury and age snipped too aggressively at his enthusiasm and he was forced to call it quits.

SATURDAY 15th SEPTEMBER 2007

Forest had gained some revenge on their play-off killers Yeovil Town during the summer by signing the Glovers pair of Arron Davies and Chris Cohen, and while Davies' career never took off at the City Ground, Cohen would become a key feature of the team, making an impressive debut at Port Vale in a 2-0 League Two victory. An industrious, all-action midfielder with an eye for presenting an opportunity to a team-mate, Cohen had made a handful of appearances for West Ham United before moving to Yeovil in 2006. He won Forest's Player of the Year award after a blistering 2008/09 campaign.

SATURDAY 16th SEPTEMBER 1905

A young Enoch 'Knocker' West made his debut for the club in a 3-2 league win against Bury at the City Ground. Born in Nottinghamshire, in Hucknall Tonkard, West had begun his career at Sheffield United but joined Forest in 1905 for £5 after failing to start a game for the Blades. Forest got themselves a versatile striker who linked well with Grenville Morris, and West finished the season with 14 goals despite Forest's relegation. His star began to shine as Forest won the second division in 1906/07, and it began to eclipse even Morris's as he scored 50 top-flight goals over the next two seasons. In 1910 he moved to Manchester United and won a league championship winners' medal with them that season, but it all went wrong for him in 1915 as he was banned for life along with team-mates Sandy Turnbull and Arthur Whalley, plus Liverpool's Jackie Sheldon, Tom Miller, Bob Pursell and Tom Fairfoul, for allegedly fixing a game between the sides. West would further suffer for repeatedly stating his innocence, even going as far as suing the FA, as the others had their ban lifted in 1919 (Turnbull posthumously) for serving their country in the First World War. West's ban was eventually lifted in 1945, by which time he was 59. West passed away in September 1965.

SUNDAY 16th SEPTEMBER 1900

Long-serving right-back Bill Thompson was born in Derby. On the cusp of his career and with an England Schoolboy cap in his locker, Thompson's progress was halted by the outbreak of war, and he went to work for Rolls-Royce, turning out for their highly-regarded works team alongside future Derby County legend George Thornwell. Both Thornwell and Thompson would sign for Forest after the war but, while Thornwell moved swiftly to the Baseball Ground, Thompson was retained longer, making his debut in 1922. He was a rugged and determined player but fair, and was the obvious choice to succeed Bob Wallace as captain in 1930. Thompson retired from playing in 1935.

SATURDAY 17th SEPTEMBER 1977

Peter Shilton made his Nottingham Forest debut against Aston Villa at the City Ground a day before his 29th birthday. Fittingly and tellingly, he kept a clean sheet.

MONDAY 17th SEPTEMBER 1979

Peter Taylor denied that £1 million man Trevor Francis was being shown the door at Nottingham Forest. 'Trevor Francis will stay at this club as long as Brian Clough and I are in charge,' he inaccurately predicted. 'It's unbelievable that anyone could think otherwise – but there appears to be a campaign, which disgusts and angers me.'

WEDNESDAY 18th SEPTEMBER 1957

Newly-promoted Forest rode on the back of their promotion momentum by beating Burnley 7-0 at the City Ground, gaining the league's top spot for the first time in living memory. All five forwards scored for the Reds – Billy Gray, Jim Barrett, Stewart Imlach (2), Tommy Wilson (2) and Eddie Baily. Forest's good form would last for two more weeks before four successive defeats saw them plummet from the summit, although they would still finish the season in a very respectable tenth place.

SATURDAY 18th SEPTEMBER 1982

Brian Clough's hands-on approach to hooliganism was demonstrated again as he frogmarched a pitch invader – half-heartedly dressed as a clown – from the field of play during Forest's 2-0 win over Watford at the City Ground. Fast forward a decade and Clough's attitude had taken a complete reverse, as he marched 11 clowns onto the pitch every Saturday for Forest's latest demise as they hurtled out of the top flight.

TUESDAY 18th SEPTEMBER 2007

Forest goalkeeper Paul Smith achieved something no Forest custodian had achieved prior to him by scoring in a match. This goal came with a caveat though, as it wasn't a typical wind-assisted punt, penalty or last minute finish. The game in which it occurred was a Carling Cup second round tie against Leicester City. This was a replay of an abandoned game which had taken place three weeks earlier which was halted at half-time when the Foxes' Clive Clarke fell dangerously ill. As Forest were 1-0 up at the time of the abandonment Leicester extremely sportingly allowed Smith to gentle dribble the ball up the pitch and stroke it into the net as soon as the replay kicked off.

TUESDAY 19th SEPTEMBER 1961

The City Ground switched on its new floodlights for the first time for a league game with an evening encounter with Wolverhampton Wanderers. The Forest side were suitably enlightened, enjoying a 3-1 victory with goals by Colin Booth, 'Flip' Le Flem and Geoff Vowden…

SATURDAY 19th SEPTEMBER 1964

…who played his last game for the club against Fulham in a 3-2 defeat at the City Ground, in which he scored. The popular Channel Islander lost his place due to the arrivals of Frank Wignall and John Barnwell, and was sold to Birmingham City for £16,000.

SATURDAY 19th SEPTEMBER 1981

A surprise team selection for Forest at Stoke City as the number 11 shirt was unexpectedly occupied by Colin Walsh as opposed to its owner for the past six years, John Robertson. What's even more surprising is that Walsh hadn't even travelled to the Potteries with Forest. It turned out that Robertson had handed in a transfer request before the game and was immediately sent home, while Walsh was phoned up as the Scotsman's replacement and arrived at the Victoria Ground a mere half-an-hour before kick-off.

WEDNESDAY 19th SEPTEMBER 1990

Forest announced the capture of a World Cup finalist, the Argentine defender Nestor Lorenzo, who played for his country in the 1990 World Cup final. This turned out to be a deal that never was, as it fell though, Lorenzo instead joining his compatriot Ossie Ardiles, then the manager of Swindon Town. Lorenzo would play 27 times for Swindon in two seasons before returning to Argentina in 1992.

WEDNESDAY 20th SEPTEMBER 1967

Forest won a European tie for the first time, beating Eintracht Frankfurt in the first round of the 1967/68 Inter-Cities Fairs Cup with a 1-0 win in Germany thanks to a Joe Baker goal. Forest went on to take the tie, winning 4-0 at the City Ground a fortnight later.

SATURDAY 20th SEPTEMBER 1986

The Reds followed up their 6-0 thrashing of Aston Villa at the City Ground the previous Saturday with an even more impressive demolition of Chelsea at Stamford Bridge, winning 6-2 despite being 2-1 down at one stage. Neil Webb and Garry Birtles both scored hat-tricks, Webb bringing his season's tally to ten in seven games, Birtles seven in the same number.

MONDAY 20th SEPTEMBER 2004

One of the saddest days in Forest's history when news came through that their legendary former manager Brian Clough had passed away at Derby City Hospital, succumbing to stomach cancer at the age of 69. Since leaving the Forest hot-seat in 1993 Clough had suffered from poor health, requiring a liver transplant in January 2003, but his death came as a sizeable shock. A memorial service was planned at Derby Cathedral, but such was the overwhelming demand for tickets that it was held instead at Derby County's Pride Park Stadium. A crowd of 14,000 turned up to pay tribute to the man whose footballing brain had brought success to both the Rams and the Reds and joy to untold thousands of supporters. In August 2005 the stretch of the A52 which links Nottingham and Derby was renamed 'Brian Clough Way', and in 2008 a statue of Clough was unveiled in Nottingham city centre. Since 2007 the Brian Clough Trophy has been played for by Forest and Derby, awarded to whoever wins any league, cup or friendly match between the two sides.

SATURDAY 21st SEPTEMBER 1929

Left-back Jimmy Barrington made his debut for the Reds in a 2-2 draw at Millwall. The Lancashire-born defender was playing for Wigan Borough when he wrote to Forest in 1929 for a trial, and he impressed sufficiently to be signed up. Jimmy was a slight but dedicated player who possessed a hard shot and became tremendously popular with the support – when he was released in 1936 after well over 200 games with the club there was such an outcry he was reinstated. After his retirement a season later he settled in the Ruddington area and scouted for the club until the late 1950s. Jimmy passed away in 1968.

BRIAN CLOUGH, THE BRILLIANT MANAGER WHO GAVE NOTTINGHAM FOREST THE BEST YEARS OF THE CLUB'S HISTORY, SADLY PASSED AWAY ON 20TH SEPTEMBER 2004

SATURDAY 21st SEPTEMBER 1963

Newly-appointed Johnny Carey had made a superb impact at the club, and he guided his side to the top of the First Division following a fifth successive victory, win number five coming over Bolton Wanderers at the City Ground.

MONDAY 22nd SEPTEMBER 1952

A debut for Bobby McKinlay in a 2-0 defeat to Sheffield United in Division Two, his first appearance of a 20-year career of more than 700 games. Forest's all-time longest-serving player was born in Lochgelly on the 10th of October 1932, and was playing for Bowhill Rovers when recommended to the club by his uncle, the ex-Forest defender Billy McKinlay. Bobby had to wait patiently for a place in the side, but once centre-half Horace Gager had retired McKinlay found a natural home in the red number five shirt. He was appointed club captain in 1962, and between the 25th of April 1959 and the 14th of December 1968 McKinlay only missed one league game. Despite this consistency and continual plaudits for his work in thwarting centre forwards, he was puzzlingly overlooked by a succession of Scotland managers. Bob coached with Forest for a while after his retirement in 1970, then became a prison officer. A true Forest great and a gentleman, Bobby sadly passed away in August 2002.

SATURDAY 22nd SEPTEMBER 1951

An injury crisis meant a surprise recall for groundsman and 'A' team manager Bob McCall, who'd retired from first-team duties at the end of the 1949/50 season, for a game which ended 1-1 at Brentford. Bob was signed from Worksop Town in 1935, taking the left-back berth 172 times for Forest despite losing the prime of his career to the war.

TUESDAY 23rd SEPTEMBER 1980

The Reds set their record League Cup score by defeating the league's bottom side, Bury, 7-0 at Gigg Lane. The scoreline flattered Forest a bit, the Reds scoring twice in the dying moments of the game, and Bury also missed a penalty. Raimondo Ponte scored three, with the other goals coming from Gary Mills, Viv Anderson and Garry Birtles.

SATURDAY 24th SEPTEMBER 1960

Forest finally appointed a replacement for long-serving manager Billy Walker in the form of Andy Beattie, who had been the first manager of the Scottish national team. Successful in the lower leagues with Barrow and Stockport County, Walker rescued Huddersfield Town from Division Two and jointly managed Scotland and Forest for a time before resigning his international post in November 1960 to concentrate on the Reds. Beattie surprisingly resigned at the end of the 1962/63 season, having guided Forest to a finishing place of ninth in the top flight, their best finish since 1908.

SATURDAY 25th SEPTEMBER 1976

Carlisle United were hammered 5-1 by Brian Clough's fast-improving young side in a Division Two game at the City Ground. Peter Withe scored on his debut and Terry Curran missed a penalty. This was one of a series of successive high-scoring home games, starting with Hereford United (4-3), followed by Carlisle, Sheffield United (6-1) and Blackburn Rovers (3-0).

SATURDAY 26th SEPTEMBER 1953

Versatile forward Ronald 'Tot' Leverton played his final game for the club before being transferred to Notts County in a 3-1 defeat to Fulham at Craven Cottage. This move came at a surprising time, as 'Tot' had finally established himself as the club's centre forward after years of deputising for Forest's more established forwards. He spent three seasons at Meadow Lane before joining Walsall in 1956.

SATURDAY 27th SEPTEMBER 1913

Bury beat Forest 1-0 at Gigg Lane, condemning the Reds to their 14th successive league defeat. A week later a John Derrick goal would halt the run, earning a 1-1 draw with Huddersfield Town.

SATURDAY 27th SEPTEMBER 1952

The City Ground crowd were treated to a high-scoring game, with the Reds defeating Swansea Town 6-4. The Forest scorers were Wally Ardron (2), Jack Burkitt, Alan Moore (2) and Colin Collindridge.

TUESDAY 28th SEPTEMBER 1965

The club's centenary celebrations continued with the official centenary match against Valencia. A crowd of 18,922 braved the rain and were delighted when Chris Crowe scored from the penalty spot after just three minutes, the penalty awarded after right-back Verdugo handballed. Valencia equalised after 19 minutes when Vicente Guillot brushed aside two tackles to hit the ball past Peter Grummitt and then head home after the ball bounced back off the post. The game ended 1-1.

SATURDAY 28th SEPTEMBER 1985

Neil Webb found himself in goal for 77 minutes in a game at Upton Park after keeper Hans Segers was injured. West Ham United were already 2-0 up, and made it 3-0 soon after Webb took over between the sticks. It was 4-0 after an hour, then Johnny Metgod and Nigel Clough scored to give the score some respectability.

SATURDAY 29th SEPTEMBER 1962

The Reds took the lead in a game at White Hart Lane after five minutes through Trevor Hockey – only to eventually lose by an embarrassing 9-2 scoreline. Geoff Vowden scored Forest's second four minutes from time, sandwiching goals from Jimmy Greaves (4), Cliff Jones (2), John White, Terry Medwin and Les Allen. Jimmy Greaves always enjoyed playing against Forest, scoring 24 league goals against them.

SATURDAY 30th SEPTEMBER 1959

Forest travelled to Paisley to complete an unofficial tie with St Mirren, a challenge match between the current England and Scotland FA Cup holders. It was the first time the team had ever travelled by air to a game. Forest were already 3-2 down from the first leg, and a 2-2 draw at Love Street meant they returned defeated.

SATURDAY 30th SEPTEMBER 1979

A 2-1 win over Aston Villa saw Forest equal Leeds United's top-flight record of 34 games unbeaten. Tommy Craig gave Villa the lead from the spot, only for Tony Woodcock and John Robertson (also a penalty) to score to preserve Forest's run.

NOTTINGHAM FOREST
On This Day

OCTOBER

SATURDAY 1st OCTOBER 1921

A 3-0 victory over Derby County at the City Ground saw Forest notch a record seventh successive victory in their new Division Two campaign following relegation the previous season. Having lost their first game 4-1 at Crystal Palace, it had been 100% for the Reds ever since. The scorers against the Rams were Walter Tinsley, Jack Spaven and Bobby Parker.

SATURDAY 1st OCTOBER 1977

The latest recruitment to Brian Clough's surging squad, Archie Gemmill, was handed a debut in a 1-1 draw at home to Norwich City in place of Ian Bowyer. Afterwards, he was criticised by his reacquainted boss and instantly dropped from the team for spending the entire match passing the ball sideways.

SATURDAY 2nd OCTOBER 1967

Forest fell 1-0 to Hull City, for whom new signing and Leeds legend Billy Bremner scored on his debut with a free kick. This game contained no less than five disallowed goals – three for the Tigers and two for Forest – who had loan signing Larry Lloyd making his debut following his temporary move from Coventry City.

SUNDAY 2nd OCTOBER 1983

Live coverage of football on TV returned after an absence of nearly quarter of a century (there was a failed experiment on ITV in the 1960/61 season) as viewers were treated to a decent match at White Hart Lane between Tottenham Hotspur and Forest. Colin Walsh gave Forest the lead after five, and Spurs were second-best until the second half, when Gary Stevens headed in Garry Brooke's cross. With five minutes to go Brooke's free kick was headed downwards by Mark Falco for Steve Archibald to prod the ball past Hans van Breukelen.

SATURDAY 3rd OCTOBER 1896

Who says hooliganism is a modern blight? A game at Derby County between Forest and the Rams was abandoned after 70 minutes when supporters invaded the pitch with the scoreline at 1-1. The game was replayed six weeks later with Derby coming out on top with a 2-1 victory.

THURSDAY 3rd OCTOBER 1912

Forest were without centre forward Jack Allan for a game at home to Barnsley, as he was a schoolteacher and was unable to get the time off work to play! Forest managed without him anyway, winning 2-0 thanks to a goal from John Derrick and a penalty from Syd Gibson.

TUESDAY 4th OCTOBER 1977

Peter Withe, who'd started the 1977/78 season with five goals in the first five games, broke a three-game scoring duck and returned to his goal-a-game average by netting four against Ipswich Town at the City Ground. Forest's 4-0 win sent them back to the top of the First Division table, and Withe became the first Forest man to score four goals in a match since Tommy Wilson 20 years earlier.

THURSDAY 4th OCTOBER 1990

The sad news came through that Brian Clough's eternal right-hand man, Peter Taylor, had suddenly passed away while holidaying in Majorca, at the age of 62. The former inseparable pals hadn't spoken since 1983 following Taylor's return to Derby and the signing of John Robertson, but reportedly Clough still cried heavily when told the news. Clough dedicated his 1994 autobiography to Taylor, saying 'To Peter. Still miss you badly. You once said: 'When you get shot of me there won't be as much laughter in your life.' You were right.'

SATURDAY 5th OCTOBER 1957

Billy Walker handed a debut to Scottish inside-forward John Quigley, who scored to give Forest a 4-3 victory over Tottenham Hotspur at White Hart Lane. Quigley had failed to make the grade at Celtic, journeying down to England to join Forest in July 1957, and made the number eight shirt his own from his debut game onwards. In 1959 Quigley scored the goal in the FA Cup semi-final against Aston Villa that sent Forest to Wembley, and he took home a cup winners' medal nearly two months later. Quigley lost his place to the likes of Colin Addison and John Barnwell in 1964 and moved to Huddersfield Town in February 1956, later playing for Bristol City and Mansfield Town. Johnny passed away in November 2004.

SATURDAY 5th OCTOBER 2002

David Johnson scored twice in a 2-1 win at Millwall, completing a scoring sequence of six successive games. That brought his total so far for the season to 13 goals in 12 league games, a complete turnaround to his previous injury-ravaged form since signing from Ipswich in January 2001. Johnson would end the season with a marvellous total of 29 goals, easily his best tally in a Forest shirt. Injury forced his retirement in 2007.

WEDNESDAY 6th OCTOBER 1948

Laurence 'Larry' Valentine Lloyd was born in Bristol. A classic Cloughie signing, Lloyd had reached the dizzying heights of league championship wins and England caps in the early 1970s with Liverpool, before the emergence of Phil Thompson saw him sold to Coventry City for a record fee of £240,000 at the start of the 1974/75 season. In truth, the Sky Blues couldn't really afford the outlay and, after Lloyd continued on a slight downward spiral, they cut their losses and sold him to Forest for a bargain £60,000 in 1976. For the next four seasons Lloyd played the best football of his career, forming a deadly partnership with Kenny Burns and earning his fourth and final England cap in 1980 against Wales, although his performance in that game reportedly caused Clough to congratulate Lloyd on winning two caps on the same day ('your first and your last'). Lloyd left Forest in March 1981 to become player-manager of Wigan Athletic, moving on to Notts County in 1983. He took the Magpies very temporarily to the league's top spot, but this turned out to be quite a false dawn as the club were relegated at the end of the season and Lloyd was sacked in October 1984.

SATURDAY 6th OCTOBER 1951

Tommy Wilson made his debut for the Reds against Luton Town at the City Ground in a 2-0 win. Originally an outside-right, it took time for him to establish himself in the side, and then it was only at centre forward once Ron Blackman had failed as Wally Ardron's replacement. Wilson proved to be a much greater success in the number nine shirt, leading Forest's forward line with a regular supply of goals and scoring in the 1959 FA Cup final. Wilson lost his place in 1960 and moved onto Walsall for a couple of seasons before retiring. Tommy passed away in 1992.

SATURDAY 7th OCTOBER 1978

Nottingham Forest confirmed their place as the current dominating force of English football by beating Wolves 3-1 at the City Ground to record their 35th consecutive league game without defeat, setting a new record for the top flight.

FRIDAY 7th OCTOBER 1988

Brian Clough rescued Lee Chapman from his French nightmare by bringing him back to English football from Chamois Niortais, for whom he'd signed from Sheffield Wednesday just over four months previously. The transfer was held up by the Football League as the Owls were still owed money by the French side, but Chapman was cleared to don a red shirt once successful negotiations had taken place. Chapman's spell at Forest would only last 14 months, during which he scored 27 goals in 71 games, before he was sold to Leeds in January 1990 for £400,000. He went on to win a league championship winners' medal with United in 1992.

TUESDAY 8th OCTOBER 1985

Winger Steve Wigley made his final appearance for the club in a 3-0 Milk Cup win at Bolton Wanderers before being sold to Sheffield United. Wigley had burst onto the scene in 1983 as an old-fashioned right-winger who relied upon an array of tricks and his dribbling skills to bypass opposition full-backs, but his initial impetus faded and the emergence of speedster Franz Carr saw him fall from the first-team picture. He moved onto Birmingham City from United, and then Portsmouth and Exeter City. Wigley then had one of the briefest top-flight managerial careers of all time, taking charge of Southampton for 14 games in 2004.

THURSDAY 8th OCTOBER 1987

Brian Clough made one of his surprise transfer signings in picking up totally unknown Doncaster Rovers striker Tommy Gaynor for £25,000. The Irishman took his chance in the limelight and performed magnificently whenever called upon, including in the 1989 Littlewoods Cup final against Luton Town. He scored a memorable goal against Huddersfield Town in the same competition later that year, collecting the ball in his own penalty area before dribbling the entire length of the pitch and firing home from 20 yards.

SATURDAY 9th OCTOBER 1965

Youngster David Wilson scored the fifth and final goal without reply in a brilliant Forest win over West Ham United at the City Ground. In doing so, he became the first Forest substitute to score in a game. Wilson had replaced Alan Hinton (who'd scored the fourth goal) earlier in the match. He left for Carlisle United later that season, then played for Grimsby Town, Walsall, Burnley and Chesterfield.

SATURDAY 9th OCTOBER 1976

Christ the King defeated Claremont 3-2 in the Forest Bowl, a competition for local schools organised by Forest with the final played at the City Ground. Future Notts County and Coventry City skipper Brian Kilcline scored twice for Christ the King, and future Red Calvin Plummer appeared for Claremont, along with Ian Benjamin, who went on to make more than 450 league appearances, mainly for Northampton Town and Southend United.

SATURDAY 10th OCTOBER 1937

Dave 'Boy' Martin scored against Chesterfield in a 2-2 draw at the City Ground, the eighth successive game in which he had found the net. A record signing of £7,000 in 1936 from Wolverhampton Wanderers (who in turn had paid £5,000 to Belfast Celtic for the prolific Irishman in 1934), Martin had spent his childhood in an orphanage before joining the Royal Ulster Rifles as a drummer boy, earning the 'Boy' nickname that remained with him for the rest of his life. A talented but temperamental centre forward who seldom saw eye-to-eye with management, Martin scored 46 goals in 84 games with Forest before moving to Notts County in 1938. He served in World War II and was badly injured in 1944 in the invasion of Normandy, but recovered to continue his career with Ballymoney and Ballymena. Dave passed away in January 1991.

SATURDAY 10th OCTOBER 1981

£1 million man Justin Fashanu finally broke his goalscoring duck with a goal at Middlesbrough in a 1-1 draw. It was his ninth league game since his expensive and protracted signing from Norwich City. Fashanu would go on to score only four league goals all season, his last coming against Arsenal in November.

SATURDAY 11th OCTOBER 1975

A tame 0-0 draw at Fulham marked the end of George Lyall's Forest career after more than three seasons at the City Ground. The Scot had been signed from Preston North End for the start of the 1972/73 season and had provided sterling service on the right wing for much of the early 1970s. He was mooted as a candidate for Scotland's 1974 World Cup squad. The emergence of Terry Curran and the increase in promise of Martin O'Neill meant someone had to be sacrificed in Forest's midfield, and Lyall was sold to Hull City. This game also marked striker David Sunley's only game for Forest.

THURSDAY 12th OCTOBER 1911

A young Forest side took on the current champions of Canada, Hillhurst Athletic, who were on tour in England. The Reds win 4-1, with J R Blythe scoring a hat-trick. Blythe was given his league debut in the following game at Chelsea, but it turned out to be his only appearance for the Reds.

SATURDAY 12th OCTOBER 1957

Forest opened their new East Stand at the City Ground just in time to welcome 'The Busby Babes' as opponents in a League Division One meeting. A new record crowd of 47,804 turned up to watch as Forest went down 2-1, Stewart Imlach scoring for Forest, Dennis Viollet and Billy Whelan for United.

SATURDAY 13th OCTOBER 1883

Sheffield F. C. were the second visitors of the season to the Lenton Ground to take on the Forest Football Club. They took the lead, only to capitulate totally and lose 9-1. Tinsley Lindley, in only his second appearance for the Nottingham side, scored seven times.

MONDAY 13th OCTOBER 1980

The gulf between the Football League and the American version of it was firmly displayed as an under-strength Forest side took on Tampa Bay Rowdies at the City Ground and ran out 7-1 winners. The scorers were Gary Mills (3), David Needham (2), Raimondo Ponte and Kenny Burns.

SATURDAY 13th OCTOBER 2001

Craig Westcarr became Forest's youngest-ever league player when he made his debut as a substitute in Forest's 1-0 home win over Burnley, at the age of 16 years and 257 days. He wasted a glorious chance to score in his first game – played clean through, he ran half the pitch only to shoot tamely at Nikolaos Michopoulos. Westcarr moved on to Cambridge United in 2005 and Kettering Town a year later before re-emerging as a successful league player with Notts County in 2009.

SATURDAY 14th OCTOBER 1961

Brian Laws was born in Newcastle's Wallsend district. The right-back signed as an apprentice with Burnley in 1979 before climbing up the leagues with Huddersfield Town and Middlesbrough and then signing for Forest in 1988 for £120,000. Laws was a Ronnie Fenton signing and, as with the likes of Garry Parker, Nigel Jemson and John Sheridan, seemed to need to go that extra yard to convince Clough he was worthy of a place in the side. It took him until December to do so, when the absence of Des Walker saw the usual number two Steve Chettle shifted to the centre of defence, and Laws never looked back, becoming Forest's finest right-back since Viv Anderson. He served the club excellently for six seasons, until he was released and joined Grimsby Town in 1993. At Grimsby he began his successful managerial career which also saw him take the reins at Scunthorpe United, Sheffield Wednesday and Burnley.

SATURDAY 14th OCTOBER 1967

A new record attendance for the City Ground was set when the George Best-led Manchester United arrived to take on Johnny Carey's attractive side. 49,946 people enjoyed a Forest victory as the Reds stormed to a 3-1 win thanks to a brace from Joe Baker and one from Frank Wignall. Best scored the Red Devils' consolation effort.

THURSDAY 15th OCTOBER 1970

Matt Gillies continued his policy of selling established Forest stars by transferring midfielder Henry Newton to Everton for £115,000 plus the Toffeemen's Tommy Jackson.

FOREST'S LONG-SERVING UTILITY PLAYER, IAN BOWYER, MADE HIS DEBUT AGAINST BLACKPOOL ON 20TH OCTOBER 1973

SATURDAY 16th OCTOBER 1982

Kenny Swain made his debut for the club in a 1-1 draw at home to Birmingham City after signing on loan from Aston Villa as cover for the injured Viv Anderson. Previously a Chelsea striker, Swain had been converted to a right-back whilst at Villa Park where he had won championship and European Cup winners' medals. Once Anderson returned the deal was made permanent as Swain moved instead to the left flank, where he'd remain the club's regular number three until the signing of Stuart Pearce. He joined Portsmouth in 1985, then Crewe in 1988, with whom he ended his career. Swain had a brief spell in charge at Wigan Athletic for the 1993/94 season, then joined the England set -up as Under-16s manager in 2004.

SATURDAY 16th OCTOBER 1999

David Platt set a record by becoming the first Forest manager to be sent off in a game, earning his marching orders in the last minute of a match at Bramall Lane. Platt's sin was a crude tackle on Sheffield United's Paul Devlin, the same player whom Nigel Quashie had elbowed just before half-time to also see red. The nine men of Forest ended up on the wrong end of a 2-1 scoreline, having been ahead at one stage thanks to a Dougie Freedman goal.

TUESDAY 17th OCTOBER 1978

Brian Clough complained about the more boisterous elements of the Forest support, claiming he was sick and tired of their behaviour. 'All they could do was chant abuse and obscenities at opposing players and fans instead of getting behind the team,' he said.

WEDNESDAY 17th OCTOBER 1979

Forest players provided four of the goals as England beat Northern Ireland 5-1 at Windsor Park in a European Championship qualifier. Trevor Francis opened the scoring after 18 minutes, and Tony Woodcock doubled the lead after 34 minutes with his first international goal. In the second half Francis made it 3-1 just after the hour mark, then Woodcock made it 4-1 on 71, before Jimmy Nicholl completed the mauling with an own-goal three minutes later. Forest's Peter Shilton made his own slight contribution to the scoreline, failing to save Vic Moreland's 50th minute penalty.

WEDNESDAY 18th OCTOBER 1978

The Reds finally got to play against genuine foreign opposition in the European Cup after seeing off Liverpool in the first round, beating Greek champions AEK Athens 2-1 away thanks to goals by John McGovern and Garry Birtles. A dubious penalty scored by Constadinou Tassos after Kenny Burns was adjudged to have brought down Thomas Mavros kept AEK's interest in the trophy.

TUESDAY 18th OCTOBER 2005

Undoubtedly one of Forest's poorest performances of all time as the former European champions went down by the odd goal in five in the LDV Vans Trophy to non-league Woking in front of a pitiful 3,127 spectators at the Kingfield Stadium. Mark Rawle gave the Conference side an unexpected lead after 10 minutes but goals by Eugen Bopp and Spencer Weir-Daley saw Gary Megson's youthful Forest side ahead. Eight minutes into the second half Rawle scored his second, then with 25 to go Justin Richards edged the non-leaguers ahead. Forest had no answer to Woking's third goal and crashed out.

WEDNESDAY 19th OCTOBER 1983

Colin Walsh scored a last minute penalty to enable Forest to take home a quite unexpected 2-1 lead from Holland against PSV Eindhoven in the first leg of the second round of the UEFA Cup. Hardly the favourites for the game, Peter Davenport had given Forest a shock lead after 51 minutes. PSV fought back and achieved parity for five minutes when Jurrie Koolhof scored a penalty after 85 minutes, before Walsh's last-gasp spot-kick.

FRIDAY 20th OCTOBER 1972

Forest fans were relieved to hear that Matt Gillies had been sacked as manager. The previously-successful Leicester City boss had taken over from Johnny Carey in February 1969 and the club had been on a downward spiral ever since, selling such stars as Terry Hennessey, Henry Newton, Joe Baker and Ian Storey-Moore and replacing them with lesser talents. Forest's failure to set the Second Division on fire at the start of the 1972/73 season signalled the end of Gillies' awful reign.

SATURDAY 20th OCTOBER 1973

Ian Bowyer was handed his debut for Forest in an eventful game at Blackpool in Division Two, starting a career at the City Ground that would last almost 14 years. Bowyer had burst onto the scene at Manchester City in 1969 as a young sharp-shooter, but once the goals dried up he became the target for boo-boys and moved on to Orient in 1971, re-inventing himself as a left-winger. During his time at Forest Bowyer played every position imaginable, including goalkeeper, and amassed more than 500 games, despite spending the years between 1978 and 1981 as a squad player and a period at Sunderland between 1981 and 1982. He was appointed club captain in the mid-1980s and settled down as a defensive midfielder, until being released in 1987. He moved into management with Hereford United in the same year, then coached for several clubs – including Forest – between 2002 and 2005. On Bowyer's Forest debut the Reds were 2-0 down and looked to be heading for a hiding, especially when goalie Jim Barron went off to be replaced by striker John Galley. However, goals by Duncan McKenzie and Bowyer himself saw them grab an unlikely point.

WEDNESDAY 20th OCTOBER 1976

Steve Burke became Forest's youngest ever first-team player when he came on as a sub for Martin O'Neill in the Anglo-Scottish Cup tie at home to Ayr United, just 22 days after his 16th birthday. It would be Burke's only game for the Reds, as he was sold to Queens Park Rangers for £125,000 three years later without troubling the first team again.

SATURDAY 21st OCTOBER 1961

Jack Burkitt made his record 463rd and final league appearance for Nottingham Forest in a Division One match at Manchester City at the age of 35, bringing down the curtain on his 15-year Forest career.

TUESDAY 21st OCTOBER 2008

There was a new goalkeeper for the Reds in Lee Camp, signed on loan from Queens Park Rangers. The consistent Camp would go on to be a massive hit between the sticks for Forest, signing permanently in the 2008/09 close season.

THE REDS' ENIGMATIC MIDFIELDER PLAYMAKER, LEWIS MCGUGAN, SCORED A MEMORABLE 35-YARD FREE KICK ON 22ND OCTOBER 2010

THURSDAY 22nd OCTOBER 2009

Forest and Derby County were fined a total of £50,000 for failing to control their players after Forest's 3-2 win at the City Ground on 29th August. At the end of the game Forest winger Nathan Tyson had removed a corner flag and paraded it in front of the Derby County supporters, sparking a melee that involved both players and staff. Tyson himself was fined £5,000 and given a two-match suspended ban.

FRIDAY 22nd OCTOBER 2010

Talented Forest midfield man Lewis McGugan scored one of the best free kicks ever seen at the City Ground against Ipswich Town. On the stroke of half-time Grant Leadbitter fouled Chris Cohen 35 yards out from goal. McGugan took a six-yard run-up and fired a missile that swerved around the two-man wall before exploding into the top right corner of Marton Fulop's goal. Forest won the game 2-0.

SATURDAY 23rd OCTOBER 1971

The idea that this was likely to be a season of struggle for Nottingham Forest was confirmed when they travelled to White Hart Lane for a league match and were soundly beaten 6-1, marking their 13th successive league match without a win. It was a debut to forget for young striker Alan Buckley, who went on to have a notable career as a prolific marksman and eventually a manager in the lower divisions, and it was only fledgling goalkeeper Eric Hulme's second league appearance. Paul Richardson scored Forest's consolation effort.

TUESDAY 23rd OCTOBER 1973

A shock for Forest as, after a 0-0 draw at home to Hull City, manager Dave Mackay announced he had accepted the offer to take over from Clough and Taylor at Derby County after Ipswich Town's Bobby Robson had turned down the chance to seize the reins at the Baseball Ground. This came as a bitter blow to the Reds, who had begun the season well – young striker Duncan McKenzie seemed especially inspired by Mackay's presence. Mackay would add Bruce Rioch and Franny Lee to the squad assembled by Clough and Taylor, and guide Derby to the title in 1974/75.

WEDNESDAY 24th OCTOBER 1979

Early strikes by forward pair Tony Woodcock and Garry Birtles were enough for Forest to take a 2-0 victory over the Romanian side Arges Pitesti in their latest success in their second European Cup campaign.

SATURDAY 24th OCTOBER 1998

Youthful Liverpool striker Michael Owen showed the goal-shy Forest frontline (so far that season only one Forest striker, Jean-Claude Darcheville, had found the net – twice) how to go about it by scoring four in a league match at Anfield. Owen gave his side the lead after ten minutes, and although Dougie Freedman had equalised with his first of the season eight minutes later, it was one-way traffic from that moment onwards. Owen scored his second on 38, completed his hat-trick with a penalty on 71 and made it four on 77. A goal from Steve McManaman on 23 added to the rout.

TUESDAY 25th OCTOBER 1977

The previous season, local rivals Forest and Notts County were very much on a par in their battle for promotion from the Second Division – a chase in which the Reds prevailed. A few months on and already it was clear table-topping Forest had taken a huge stride forwards, emphasised by a 4-0 City Ground defeat of the Magpies in the League Cup. Goals by John Robertson (penalty), Tony Woodcock and Ian Bowyer (2) saw County crash out. The game witnessed a debut for 17-year-old rookie keeper Chris Woods, called into unexpected action after John Middleton had been transferred to Derby County and with Peter Shilton being cup-tied.

SATURDAY 25th OCTOBER 1980

A rare missed game from Peter Shilton gave 19-year-old Steve Sutton the chance to make his debut in a league game at Carrow Road against Norwich City, and he performed excellently in a 1-1 draw. Sutton had to wait patiently to become Forest's regular keeper, first under studying Shilton and then Hans van Breukelen. Bizarrely, whilst still a Forest player, Sutton would become the only keeper beaten by a Des Walker strike (in the right net, anyhow), on New Year's Day 1992 when Sutton was on loan and playing against Forest for Luton Town.

SATURDAY 26th OCTOBER 1929

All-round sportsman Len Langford played his last game for the Reds in goal in a 2-0 home defeat by Charlton Athletic, in which he was injured and taken off just after the hour. As well as football, Langford made his mark in cricket, the high jump, and boxing, being middleweight champion of the Household Brigade in 1920 and 1921. Langford moved on to Manchester City in 1930. He then played in the 1933 FA Cup final, the first final in which numbers were worn, sporting the number 22 jersey. He moved to Manchester United in 1934 before retiring in 1937. He passed away in 1973.

SATURDAY 26th OCTOBER 1957

Following the previous Saturday's record 47,804 turn-out for the visit of Manchester United to the City Ground, another bumper crowd of 41,586 were on hand for the visit of Blackpool to Nottingham, who included in their ranks the legendary Stanley Matthews. It was the wizard-like wingman's first visit to Forest's ground. Just like against United, the huge attendance failed to inspire the Reds, who went down 2-1, a Jim Barrett penalty their sole strike.

SATURDAY 27th OCTOBER 1951

A 19-year-old centre-half named Bobby McKinlay made his debut for Forest, starting his record-breaking 20-year career at the City Ground. Forest's opponents were Coventry City at Highfield Road in an entertaining 3-3 draw. Forest's goals came from Noel Kelly (2) and Tommy Johnson, while Ted Roberts netted a hat-trick for the Sky Blues.

TUESDAY 27th OCTOBER 1987

After negotiating a potential banana skin against Fourth Division Hereford United in the second round of the Littlewoods Cup (6-1 on aggregate), Forest slipped up at Maine Road, tumbling out of the competition to Mel Machin's Manchester City, who then were mid-table in the second flight. Imre Varadi gave City the lead after only three minutes, an advantage Paul Stewart would double on 23. Just as it looked as if Forest were staging a fight back, Varadi scored his second on 53, and it was curtains for Brian Clough's men.

FRIDAY 28th OCTOBER 1949

John McGovern, Forest's skipper throughout the glory years of the late 1970s and early 1980s, was born in Montrose. McGovern's family moved to Hartlepool when McGovern was seven and, after excelling at both rugby and football, the youngster chose the latter and made his debut for Brian Clough's Hartlepool United side at the age of 16. By the age of 19 McGovern had played in all four divisions of the Football League (becoming the youngest player to do so), having followed Clough and Taylor to Derby County in 1968. Wherever Cloughie went McGovern would surely follow, and a transfer to Leeds United followed in 1974, and then to Forest in 1975. A steadying influence at the rear of midfield, McGovern's contribution amongst a side of flair players was seldom recognised by the Forest supporters, but one does not play nearly 600 games for Brian Clough if one is rubbish. The relationship ended in 1982 when McGovern was allowed to take over as player-manager at Bolton Wanderers. He also managed Rotherham United (jointly with Archie Gemmill) before settling into a role as co-commentator on BBC Radio Nottingham.

TUESDAY 28th OCTOBER 1980

Possibly the worst result of Brian Clough's Forest reign until then occurred when the Reds were dumped out of the League Cup by Second Division Watford, who triumphed 4-1 at Vicarage Road. Striking for Graham Taylor's rising side were Luther Blissett, who netted a penalty, and Ross Jenkins, who scored a hat-trick in 14 minutes. Ian Wallace pulled one back for Forest but, as they were already 4-0 down, it was of barely any consequence.

SATURDAY 29th OCTOBER 1977

Cloughie's Forest marched on with a 4-0 demolition of John Neal's Middlesbrough, including two dazzling goals from right-back Viv Anderson and John McGovern's first strike for four years. Forest shut up shop at 4-0 up on 55 minutes – job done.

SATURDAY 29th OCTOBER 1994

Newly-promoted Forest saw their unbeaten record of 20 games end with a 2-0 home defeat by Blackburn Rovers, Nottingham-born Chris Sutton scoring both Rovers goals.

FRIDAY 30th OCTOBER 1959

Billy Walker splashed some of the cash generated by the club's FA Cup win in May by signing Wolverhampton Wanderers striker Colin Booth for a club record fee of £20,000. Booth would only score eight goals in his first season with his new side, but the following term he tallied a far more respectable 19 in 35 league games. After the end of the 1961/62 season Booth was sold to Doncaster Rovers where he became hugely prolific (57 goals in 88 games). He went on to Oxford United and, finally, non-league Cambridge United, where he ended his career.

FRIDAY 30th OCTOBER 1998

It was announced that the club's recalcitrant forward Pierre van Hooijdonk had agreed to conclude his one-man strike while demanding an allegedly promised transfer and return to his employers. Reportedly, the reception he received from his team-mates upon his return was several degrees below lukewarm. Once restored to the basement-dwelling side, it took van Hooijdonk three games to score, and even though that goal was against fierce rivals Derby County, the other, more loyal Forest players chose to congratulate Scot Gemmill (who'd supplied the goal) rather than the once-popular Dutchman. In and out of the team for the remainder of the season, the seemingly disinterested van Hooijdonk weighed in with half-a-dozen goals as the club slid back out of the top flight with barely a whimper before eventually winning his move by being sold to Vitesse Arnhem for £3.5 million at the end of the season.

TUESDAY 31st OCTOBER 1995

Much-maligned 'pineapple-head' Jason Lee put in easily his best performance for Forest, in a 0-0 draw at Auxerre in the second leg of the second round of the UEFA Cup. Protecting a fragile 1-0 lead from the first leg, Forest went ultra-defensive. It was left to the frontman to rampage alone up front, receiving and shielding the ball as often as possible, a job his talents were perfectly tailored for. At the other end Mark Crossley, another player with more than his deserved share of critics, had the game of his life to keep the French side at bay, proving equal to everything they could throw at him.

NOTTINGHAM FOREST
On This Day

NOVEMBER

SATURDAY 1st NOVEMBER 1975

Newly-appointed Dick Young was given a rude introduction to football management when his Carlisle United side visited the City Ground and were beaten 4-0. Forest's goals came from Barry Butlin, John O'Hare (2) and Terry Curran. Young would just prevent Carlisle from suffering their second successive relegation at the end of the 1975/76 season, but was usurped by Bobby Moncur barely a year after his appointment.

WEDNESDAY 1st NOVEMBER 1978

Just as a year previously, when the First Division began to regard Forest as serious contenders for the title, the rest of Europe was forced now to regard the Reds as serious candidates to win the European Cup, after they demolished AEK Athens 5-1 at the City Ground to progress to the quarter finals 7-2 on aggregate. Goals from David Needham, Tony Woodcock, Viv Anderson and improving youngster Garry Birtles (2) saw Forest progress, with Douzo Bajevic replying.

THURSDAY 2nd NOVEMBER 1972

Forest announced the successor to Matt Gillies as manager – former Tottenham Hotspur 'hardman' and legend and then-Swindon Town manager Dave Mackay. Mackay was still only 37, and had only his time at Swindon to call upon as a manager, but nobody could quibble regarding his experience in the game. The club played out his first season quietly in mid-table, but steady progress seemed to be being made the following term. Just as Mackay introduced his new signing, Ian Bowyer, to the side, he took the chance to succeed Clough and Taylor at Derby County and his 11-month reign was over.

MONDAY 2nd NOVEMBER 1980

The club announced the sad death of Noel Watson, who had served the club in various capacities since the 1930s. He had been manager between 1931 and 1936 when the role was largely administrative, and club secretary until 1959. He moved onto the committee and was the club's president at the time of his death. Noel was also a first-class referee, taking charge of the 1925 FA Cup final between Sheffield United and Cardiff City.

THURSDAY 2nd NOVEMBER 1989

The hopes of the Forest support that £650,000 summer signing John Sheridan, inexplicably ignored by Brian Clough since his transfer, might finally get a chance to show he was capable of replacing Neil Webb in the heart of Forest's midfield were finally dashed when the Irishman was sold to Sheffield Wednesday for £500,000.

SATURDAY 3rd NOVEMBER 1956

Forest played under floodlights for the first time in a league game, at Stoke City's Victoria Ground. A crowd of 32,637 turned up to watch the Potters secure a 2-1 victory thanks to goals by Frank Bowyer and Harry Oscroft, with Doug Lishman scoring for Forest.

SUNDAY 3rd NOVEMBER 1985

Brian Clough's youthful Forest side seemed to have put their dreadful, one-win-in-six start to the season firmly behind them by recording their seventh successive win, a nervy 2-1 victory at home to West Brom through goals by Neil Webb and Peter Davenport (penalty) replying to one from Steve Hunt. The other victims during Forest's excellent run were Ipswich Town (3-1), Bolton Wanderers (LC 3-0), Aston Villa (2-0), Newcastle United (3-0), Arsenal (3-2) and Derby County (LC 2-1). The run would end the following week with a 4-2 defeat at Chelsea.

SATURDAY 4th NOVEMBER 1989

John Sheridan finally played in a league game at the City Ground following his welcome capture from Leeds United, but for Sheffield Wednesday! His distribution was a feature of an otherwise dull game, settled when Forest defender Terry Wilson attempted to hack a goal-bound effort off the line only to slam it into his own net.

SATURDAY 4th NOVEMBER 2000

The Reds won an ugly game at the City Ground against Preston North End, who were forced to play the last 20 minutes with only nine men, following the dismissals of Graham Alexander on 12 minutes for raising fists to Jack Lester, then Colin Murdock for fighting. Jon Macken had put Preston ahead, but two penalties from Chris Bart-Williams and one from Ben Olsen saw Forest win.

SATURDAY 5th NOVEMBER 1960

Billy Walker's side went down 5-3 at Wolverhampton Wanderers, their seventh successive league defeat. This latest reverse, coupled with the fact that he had conceded 26 goals in his last nine league appearances, was enough to convince Walker to drop FA Cup final goalkeeper 'Chic' Thomson and give promising youngster Peter Grummitt a chance between the sticks instead. Grummitt would be such a success that the Wolves game marked the last match Thomson would play for Forest, and he was released at the end of the season.

SATURDAY 5th NOVEMBER 2005

Another dreadful result for Forest under Gary Megson, as they were held to a 1-1 draw at the City Ground by Conference South side Weymouth in the first round of the FA Cup. It took the Reds almost the entire first half to make any sort of progress against the non-leaguers, and with barely five minutes until half-time Gary Holt coverted Nicky Southall's teasing cross. The expected avalanche wasn't forthcoming in the second half though, and ten minutes in Andy Harris equalised from Lee Elam's lofted ball. Weymouth held on to secure a replay without much difficulty.

MONDAY 6th NOVEMBER 1962

Long-time Forest skipper and servant Jack Burkitt was rewarded for his years on the staff with a testimonial against the Swedish side Malmo who, with eerie prescience, would play Forest in the final of the European Cup 17 years later. The Reds eased to a 5-1 victory in foggy conditions with a goal apiece from the entire forward line of Geoff Vowden, Colin Booth, Colin Addison, Johnny Quigley and 'Flip' Le Flem. With conditions worsening, the game was abandoned after 79 minutes.

SATURDAY 6th NOVEMBER 1993

The Iceman cometh! Norwegian signing Lars Bohinen made his debut in a 3-0 win at St Andrew's against Birmingham City. An ingenious and gifted playmaker, Bohinen would be the spark that ignited Forest's 1993/94 promotion campaign. He would remain at the club until an odd clause in his contract allowed him to join Blackburn Rovers in October 1995 for a pitiful £700,000.

SATURDAY 7th NOVEMBER 1970

Having won only one game out of the last ten, manager Matt Gillies resorted to desperate tactics for a trip to Goodison Park by chucking in young debutants Jimmy McIntosh, a right-winger signed from Montrose, and central defender John Cottam who'd risen through the Forest ranks. The introduction of the two 20-year-olds had little effect, and Forest went down 1-0 thanks to an Alan Whittle goal for Everton.

SATURDAY 8th NOVEMBER 1879

The Forest Football Club commenced their second season in the FA Cup just as they had their first the previous year, with a tie against Notts. Football Club, the team who, of course, would go on to be known as Notts County. In the battle of the local rivals it was the Forest men who emerged victorious, winning by four goals without reply. The scorers were Sam Widdowson and A. H. Smith, both bagging a brace.

TUESDAY 8th NOVEMBER 1977

There was worrying news for surprise league leaders Forest when manager Brian Clough formally declared his interest in taking over as England manager from the recently-departed Don Revie. 'They want me to stay,' he said of the Nottingham public. 'But we still have a lot of season tickets still unsold.'

SATURDAY 9th NOVEMBER 1935

Forest beat Barnsley 4-0 in a Division Two clash at the City Ground, in which inside-left Tom Peacock scored four goals. Barnsley were forced to play the last hour with only ten men after left-back Bill Anderson, who'd briefly been on Forest's books as a youngster, broke his leg. Forest's other goals came from Billy Simpson and Harry Race. This was to be the most prolific season of Tom Peacock's career, as the forward contributed 21 goals to Forest's largely lacklustre campaign, despite missing the final six weeks of the season. Peacock was a teacher before turning to professional football, and once the war had ended his career (he served as a flight sergeant in the RAF during the conflict) he returned to education, becoming headmaster of St Edmund's Primary School in Mansfield Woodhouse in 1955.

WEDNESDAY 9th NOVEMBER 1966

Johnny Carey announced the £45,000 capture of Rotherham United right-winger Barry Lyons, beating a host of other interested parties to his signature. Lyons was a Notts lad but had failed in a trial in 1962 for the club and instead moved north to Millmoor to play his football. He took over the number seven shirt from Chris Crowe and became an integral part of Forest's forward line, although he was often overshadowed by Ian Storey-Moore on the Reds' left. His commitment could never be faulted though, and he served Forest consistently until being sold to York City in September 1973 for £12,000. He moved onto Darlington in 1976 but returned to York as a coach upon his retirement, serving one season as the club's manager between March 1980 and December 1981.

SATURDAY 10th NOVEMBER 1956

Middlesbrough were that day's visitors to the City Ground, and they returned up north with a handsome 4-0 win under their belts, mainly thanks to a first league hat-trick from their 21-year-old striker, Brian Clough. For added Forest interest, Middlesbrough's goalkeeper was Peter Taylor.

SATURDAY 10th NOVEMBER 1979

A real shocker at The Dell as Southampton beat Forest 4-1, the first time Forest had lost a game by more than one goal since Arsenal had beaten them 3-0 at Highbury in September 1977. Garry Birtles popped up with Forest's only goal of the game, and Nottinghamshire-born pair Dave Watson and Phil Boyer (2) scored for the Saints, as well as Mick Channon.

WEDNESDAY 10th NOVEMBER 1982

The 15,000 or so hardy souls who braved a chilly evening at the City Ground to watch Forest take on Watford in the third round of the League Cup were treated to a ten-goal feast as the Reds slammed seven past the Hornets, who managed three of their own. Ross Jenkins had given Graham Taylor's men the lead after 11 minutes, finishing from John Barnes' flick-on of Ian Bolton's pass. From then on it was goals galore as Willie Young (19), Mark Proctor (32 and 82), Garry Birtles (40 and 43), Ian Bowyer (68) and Ian Wallace (85) all found a way past Steve Sherwood in the Watford goal.

SATURDAY 11th NOVEMBER 1933

Forest stormed to an unexpected 7-2 win against Bury at the City Ground thanks to goals from Billy Dickinson (2), Johnny Dent (2), Len Barry, Harry Race and Tommy Graham. It was the first time Forest had scored seven goals in a league game since they'd beaten South Shields by an identical scoreline in September 1927.

SATURDAY 11th NOVEMBER 2006

For once in the dim and dismal days of third tier football Forest safely found their way past a potential embarrassment by beating Yeading 5-0 in the first round of the FA Cup. The Conference South side were no match for the Reds, who strolled on to a second round meeting with the equally fearsome Salisbury Town thanks to a first-half Kris Commons hat-trick and a brace from 'Junior' Agogo.

SATURDAY 12th NOVEMBER 1960

Peter Grummitt made his league debut for the club at home to Bolton Wanderers. He'd been signed from his hometown club of Bourne Town in May, and was only 18 when given his first start after several impressive appearances for the reserves. It was an inauspicious beginning that saw him have to fish a Jim Iley backpass out of the net within the first minute, although two Colin Booth goals would help Forest salvage a 2-2 draw. Grummitt would retain the number one jersey until the 1968/69 season when injury saw Alan Hill seize his chance, and he was surprisingly sold to Sheffield Wednesday. He stayed at Hillsborough for another three seasons, remaining virtually ever-present throughout, before moving to Brighton & Hove Albion in 1973. He continued his amazing consistency before moving into non-league football with Worthing in 1977. Grummitt made three appearances for the England U23 team and remains one of the best keepers never to have been capped for his country, largely due to the consistency at the time of Gordon Banks as well as deputies such as Rod Springett, Tony Waiters and Peter Bonetti.

SATURDAY 12th NOVEMBER 1983

Striker Andy Gray made his debut for Everton against Forest at the City Ground following his £250,000 transfer from Wolverhampton Wanderers, a week after his final game for Wanderers...against Forest at the City Ground.

TUESDAY 13th NOVEMBER 1984

The City Ground hosted an England 'B' international between England and New Zealand, which the home side won 2-0. Appearing for the national team's second XI for the first time were Forest's Peter Davenport and Steve Hodge, the latter scoring the first goal of the game. Tottenham Hotspur's Gary Mabbutt netted the only other goal a minute from time.

SATURDAY 13th NOVEMBER 1992

Despite Forest's disastrous start to the season, which had seen them take a paltry ten points from the 45 on offer and sink to the bottom spot of the Premier League, Brian Clough was given a 12-month extension to his existing contract.

TUESDAY 14th NOVEMBER 1972

Viv Anderson signed professional forms for Forest ten weeks after turning 16, and became the first black player the club had had on their books. Anderson would begin to make appearances for the first team in 1974 and suffered the usual Neanderthal chanting from opposition supporters, but with the firm support of no-nonsense Brian Clough (when Anderson complained during one game that a member of the opposition was repeatedly calling him a 'black b*****d', Clough advised Anderson to go out, kick him and call him a 'white b*****d' in retaliation) he matured into a supremely talented right-back – as essential a part of the supreme late 1970s/early 1980s squad as any other member. He could tackle, run at speed and shoot from distance; arguably the best number two ever to turn out in Forest red. He served the club for a dozen years until leaving for Arsenal in 1984. He subsequently turned out for Manchester United, Sheffield Wednesday, Barnsley (including a brief spell as player-manager) and Middlesbrough.

SUNDAY 14th NOVEMBER 1982

The already fractured relationship between Brian Clough and Justin Fashanu took a further turn for the worse when Fashanu – who so far that season had not figured at all during the first 11 games – turned down a move to Derby County. Clough banned his centre forward from the City Ground forthwith.

SATURDAY 15th NOVEMBER 1941

The haphazard nature of wartime football was firmly displayed when Forest failed to turn up for a fixture at Norwich City having been put on the wrong train at Peterborough. Having managed to navigate from Nottingham to Peterborough, the players and officials then found themselves heading north. Disembarking at Louth, they found no train available to take them to Norwich, so sauntered back to their home town. The 3,000 spectators who turned up at Carrow Road had to be content with a seven-a-side exhibition game.

SATURDAY 15th NOVEMBER 1969

A 3-1 defeat at Newcastle United marked Bobby McKinlay's 614th and final appearance for Forest, creating a club record for league appearances that still stands to the present day.

SATURDAY 16th NOVEMBER 1878

The Forest Football Club played their first ever competitive fixture, having entered the Football Association Challenge Cup for the first time. Their opponents in the first round were The Notts. Football Club, with the game being played in Beeston. Forest were the underdogs for the tie, but went ahead after five minutes when F. W. Earp planted the ball in the Notts. goalmouth for J. P. Turner to convert. Ten minutes later the same player set up A. C. Goodyer to put the scarlet-shirted Forest side two goals up. Notts. pulled a goal back when J. R. B. Owen forced the ball through a scrimmage to net. In the second half A. C. Smith restored Forest's two-goal advantage following excellent work from Sam Widdowson and Goodyer. At this point tiredness overcame both teams and there was very little further action, with Forest running out 3-1 winners. Forest: Sands, E. Luntley, Caborn, Bates, Widdowson, Holroyd, Smith, Goodyer, Turner, Earp, W Luntley.

SATURDAY 16th NOVEMBER 1968

The club finally returned to the City Ground after six 'home' games at Notts County's Meadow Lane following the fire that destroyed the Main Stand (see August 24th 1968). Forest had failed to win a single one of their Meadow Lane games, and continued to struggle, losing 2-0 to Arsenal.

FRIDAY 16th NOVEMBER 1979

Tony Woodcock decided to leave the City Ground for a new adventure in West Germany, joining Cologne for a German-record fee of £650,000. 'This was the hardest decision of my life,' he said. 'My wife Carole and I felt we would like to move abroad at some stage in my career, and we believe the time is now right.' He would score 28 goals in 81 appearances for the German side before returning to England and signing for Arsenal in 1982. He then moved back to Cologne in 1986 and spent a couple more seasons there before moving to Fortuna Cologne in 1988, and retiring two years later.

THURSDAY 17th NOVEMBER 1977

Right-winger Terry Curran – who had fallen out with Peter Taylor and fallen foul of Clough and Taylor's decision that they couldn't play two out-and-out wide men in the top flight – was transferred to Derby County for £50,000. The tricky winger would then commence a journeyman career that took in spells at Southampton, Sheffield Wednesday (where he would become a huge hit), Atvidaberg (in Sweden), Sheffield United, Everton, Huddersfield Town, Panionios (in Greece), Hull City, Sunderland, Grantham Town, Grimsby Town and Chesterfield.

SATURDAY 17th NOVEMBER 1979

Alan Mullery's Brighton & Hove Albion side were the latest fall guys to have arrived at the City Ground expecting either nothing or, at the most, a point – or so everyone thought. Forest's unbeaten league record at home stretched back to April 1977, but it took an unexpected tumble when Gerry Ryan scored for the Seagulls after 11 minutes, a goal Forest couldn't fashion a reply to. After 51 games, the gargantuan run was over.

SATURDAY 18th NOVEMBER 1950

Gillingham were re-elected to the Football League at the end of the 1949/50 season after a 12-year absence, but after today's 9-2 defeat by a rampant Forest side at the City Ground they may have wished they had remained in the Southern League. Despite the nine goals, only three Forest players found the target. Tommy Capel got four, Wally Ardron claimed a hat-trick and Tommy Johnson scored a brace.

THURSDAY 18th NOVEMBER 1982

The banned Justin Fashanu decided to turn up for first-team training, despite being prohibited from doing so by Brian Clough. Clough was in no mood for a reconciliation, and called the police to have the young striker ejected.

SATURDAY 18th NOVEMBER 1995

If you're going to surrender an unbeaten run, you may as well surrender it in style. Forest travelled to Ewood Park for a league game against Blackburn as the last unbeaten side in the country, on top of a 13-game unbeaten run at the tail end of the previous season that meant avoiding defeat here would extend Forest's unbeaten run to 26. It was not to be as Blackburn embarrassed Frank Clark's side, hammering them 7-0 with goals by Mike Newell, Graeme Le Saux, Alan Shearer (3) and Lars Bohinen (2). Forest's cause wasn't helped by the dismissal of Steve Chettle after 67 minutes.

FRIDAY 19th NOVEMBER 1965

Terry Hennessey joined the ranks at the City Ground by signing from Birmingham City for £110,000. An established Welsh international, Hennessey turned out to be an inspired signing, forming a resolute half-back line alongside Bobby McKinlay and Henry Newton. He had his finest season in 1966/67 when Forest finished runners-up in the league and reached the semi-finals of the FA Cup, and he finished third in the vote for Footballer of the Year. He became Brian Clough's record signing when he joined Derby County in February 1972 for £100,000.

MONDAY 19th NOVEMBER 1975

Forest announced the appointment of Bury manager Allan Brown as successor to Dave Mackay. The Scot, who had played against Forest for Luton Town in the 1959 FA Cup final, had risen through the managerial ranks with Wigan, Luton, Torquay and finally Bury, who he successfully guided to the edge of the Third Division promotion race before moving to Forest. Brown's reign at the City Ground would last only 13 months, during which time he saw Duncan McKenzie blossom into the division's leading striker and guided Forest to the FA Cup quarter-finals.

SATURDAY 20th NOVEMBER 1976

The ugly rise of football hooliganism continued in a City Ground game between Forest and Chelsea when fighting spectators spilled onto the pitch, forcing referee D. Turner to take both teams off the field and into the dressing rooms for nearly five minutes. Normal proceedings on the pitch resulted in an entertaining 1-1 draw. Martin O'Neill scored for Forest following a one-two with Peter Withe, and Ian Britton equalised for the Blues, latching on to 'Sammy' Chapman's poor defensive clearance.

FRIDAY 20th NOVEMBER 1992

Brian Clough's latest solution to Forest's dismal displays was to re-sign midfield man Neil Webb from Manchester United for £800,000. While Webb returned from Old Trafford heavier and slower than when he left more than three years previously, his vision and distribution remained top-class and, after a settling-in period, he helped Forest to slowly rise back up the table. Sadly, an injury at the start of February robbed Forest of him for the remainder of the term.

TUESDAY 21st NOVEMBER 1984

Gary Megson called time on his non-existent Forest playing career by signing for Newcastle United, nearly four months after joining the Reds from Sheffield Wednesday. He failed to trouble the typist responsible for Forest's team sheets once.

SATURDAY 21st NOVEMBER 1959

FA Cup holders Nottingham Forest were severely thrown aside by the land's most exciting team, Harry Potts' Burnley, who triumphed 8-0 at Turf Moor on their way to winning the league title for the second time in their history. Jimmy Robson scored five goals for the Clarets in this game, with Ray Pointer (2) and Brian Pilkington completing Forest's embarrassment.

SATURDAY 22nd NOVEMBER 2003

Electric striker Marlon Harewood scored the second goal for Forest in a 2-2 draw at Wigan Athletic. It turned out to be his last goal in his last game for Forest, as the club's dire financial status necessitated his sale to West Ham United for a bargain price of £500,000 a few days later.

SATURDAY 23rd NOVEMBER 1946

The Reds were forced to play a 'home' game at Meadow Lane after the City Ground was flooded due to the Trent bursting its banks. Their opponents were Manchester City, who triumphed 1-0 thanks to a George Smith goal.

SATURDAY 23rd NOVEMBER 1935

Those Forest fans in attendance at the previous City Ground game, a 6-0 drubbing of Barnsley, were rewarded for their loyalty when Port Vale turned up and were slaughtered 9-2. For the second home game in succession Tom Peacock scored four, with the other goals from Harry Race (2), Johnny Dent (2) and Billy Simpson.

WEDNESDAY 24th NOVEMBER 1982

Justin Fashanu won his appeal with the Football League against Brian Clough's ban of him attending first-team matters at Forest, and was restored to training duties.

WEDNESDAY 24th NOVEMBER 1999

With the protracted transfer of Stern John from MLS's Columbus Crew finally completed, the Trinidad & Tobago international was cleared to make his debut against Portsmouth in the league. He made an almost instant impact, scoring after only six minutes in a 2-0 win. Mikkel Beck got the other.

SATURDAY 25th NOVEMBER 1978

The Reds travelled to Burnden Park for a league game with Bolton Wanderers and returned with a 1-0 victory thanks to John Robertson. This was the club's 42nd consecutive game without defeat – an entire season's worth of unbeaten games.

TUESDAY 25th NOVEMBER 1980

A tiny crowd of 12,246 welcomed Valencia to the City Ground for the first leg of the European Super Cup, a trophy Forest held after beating Barcelona the previous season. Ian Bowyer scored twice for the Reds but Dario Felman grabbed a crucial away goal for the Spaniards. Forest: Shilton, Anderson, F. Gray, McGovern, Lloyd, Burns, Mills, Bowyer, Ward (Ponte), Wallace, Robertson.

MONDAY 26th NOVEMBER 1883

The birth of George 'Tag' Needham in Shepshed. A wholehearted and committed centre-half, George signed for Forest in 1906 from Shepshed Albion and, after battling with George Wolfe for a first-team spot, eventually became a regular in the side in 1909. The emergence of Joe Mercer in 1911 necessitated a move to half-back for George, but he responded magnificently and from September 1911 to the outbreak of the First World War he failed to miss a single league game.

SATURDAY 27th NOVEMBER 1909

Unthinkable now, but on this day Nottingham Forest travelled to Manchester to take on FA Cup holders (and 1908 League champions) United at their Bank Street ground and won 6-2. Grenville Morris and Enoch West both completed hat-tricks for the Nottingham side, whilst Harry Halse and George Wall scored for United.

SATURDAY 27th NOVEMBER 1971

Forest's 'Sammy' Chapman was sent off just before half-time in a home game against Leeds, becoming the first Forest player to be dismissed for 32 years. The last had been George Pritty on March 25th 1939.

SATURDAY 28th NOVEMBER 1964

A sad day for everyone associated with the club when news emerged that long-serving manager Billy Walker had passed away. The former Aston Villa legend had been in poor health for some time, so his death was not unexpected, but that hardly lessened the impact of the loss of the man who'd been 'Mr Nottingham Forest' for a quarter of a century.

WEDNESDAY 28th NOVEMBER 1990

Forest's 22-match unbeaten run in the League Cup came to an end when they were defeated by the odd goal in nine in a topsy-turvy tie at Highfield Road against Coventy. The Reds had been 4-0 down at one stage, before battling back to 4-4. Steve Livingstone scored the crucial goal on 63 and an exhausted Forest couldn't find an equaliser.

VIV ANDERSON, FOREST'S BEST EVER RIGHT-BACK, BECAME TO FIRST BLACK PLAYER TO PLAY FOR ENGLAND ON 29TH NOVEMBER 1978

SATURDAY 29th NOVEMBER 1913

The 1913/14 season was perhaps the worst in Forest's history, as they finished bottom of the entire Football League. This day's game against Leeds City at Elland Road could therefore be described as the worst performance by a Forest team ever, as they were defeated 8-0. The Leeds players scoring for fun were Billy McLeod (4), Arthur Price (2), John Hampson and Jimmy Spiers. Forest were so desperate for goals, having scored only 14 in the season's 14 previous games, that they experimented with full-back Harry Jones at centre forward. It was not a success.

WEDNESDAY 29th NOVEMBER 1978

Viv Anderson made his deserved debut for England, in doing so famously becoming the first black player to represent England at full international level. He wore the number two shirt in a friendly against Czechoslovakia at Wembley which England won 1-0 thanks to a Steve Coppell goal. Anderson would go on to win 30 caps for his country, which should have been a lot more and would have been if he hadn't had to battle Liverpool's Phil Neal and Ipswich's Mick Mills for the right-back berth. Anderson also had the misfortune of selection for both the 82 and 86 England World Cup squads without playing a single match in either tournament.

TUESDAY 30th NOVEMBER 1976

A month's worth of transfer talks concluded when cash-strapped Coventry City decided to allow their record £240,000 signing, Larry Lloyd, to join Forest on a permanent basis for £60,000. Lloyd had been signed on loan to cover for the injured 'Sammy' Chapman in October but had returned to Coventry and their first team after the month was up. Clough and Taylor liked what they saw in the no-nonsense centre-back and pressed Coventry to sell, which eventually they did.

SUNDAY 30th NOVEMBER 1986

The Sunday papers reported that both Manchester United and Rangers were preparing bids, thought to be around £600,000, for Forest's fiery left-back Stuart Pearce. Thankfully for all involved with the club, the Reds' regular number three decided to stick around for another nine seasons.

NOTTINGHAM FOREST
On This Day

DECEMBER

SATURDAY 1st DECEMBER 1962

The 20-year-old Channel Islander, Richard 'Flip' Le Flem, scored what went down in history as one of the best goals ever scored by a Forest player. In a league game at the City Ground against championship-chasing Burnley, and with the score tied at one apiece, Le Flem received the ball just inside the Burnley half and proceeded to dribble past almost the entire Clarets defence before rifling the ball past Adam Blacklaw with an inch-perfect right-foot shot. The crowd stood as one to applaud Le Flem's effort for several minutes afterwards. Burnley couldn't find a way back from the goal and the score remained 2-1 to Forest.

SATURDAY 1st DECEMBER 1985

The Forest XI trudged off the pitch at half-time in a league game at home to Oxford United in the First Division trailing to an Andy Thomas goal after an awful display. Brian Clough was so incensed at his side's performance that he spent five minutes yelling at them, then ordered them back out on to the pitch five minutes before the second half was due to start. The display was hardly any better, but Forest did at least salvage a point when Peter Davenport was tripped in the box, getting up to net the penalty.

SATURDAY 2nd DECEMBER 1882

Sam Widdowson became the first Forest man to score a hat-trick in competition, grabbing four against Sheffield Heeley in the first round of the FA Challenge Cup. The other scorers for the Nottingham side were W Parr, F W Earp and H S Fletcher, sealing a 7-2 victory – Forest's best in their history in the competition.

SATURDAY 3rd DECEMBER 2005

Gary Megson took his Forest team to Chester for a second round FA Cup tie in which they were embarrassingly hammered 3-0. The cash-strapped side, who would soon cease to exist, were head and shoulders better than a team containing such experienced heads as Paul Gerrard, Danny Cullip, John Curtis, Nicky Southall, Gareth Taylor, David Johnson and Gary Holt, the latter hardly aiding matters by being sent off seven minutes before half-time for fouling Ryan Lowe in the box. Lowe scored twice, Marcus Richardson got the other.

SUNDAY 3rd DECEMBER 2006

One year on from that dreadful defeat at Chester, the TV cameras were on hand to broadcast to anyone interested to see how far the once double Euro champs has fallen. They couldn't even beat Conference South side Salisbury City. Nathan Tyson gave Forest the lead on 27 minutes during a rare period of play when Forest actually resembled a football team, but Salisbury possessed the bigger footballing heart and just past the hour non-league legend Matt Tubbs fired home after Nicky Southall had cleared Wayne Turk's volley off the line.

SUNDAY 4th DECEMBER 1977

The chances that Forest would be looking for a new manager rose when Brian Clough was interviewed for the post of the England national team. The people's choice for the award following his great success so far at Forest that term, Clough's interview turned out to be a sham, as the post had already been awarded to West Ham United's Ron Greenwood.

SATURDAY 4th DECEMBER 2004

Jack Lester made his second debut for the club after re-signing from Sheffield United for £50,000. The Sheffield-born forward had previously been released by the club in 2003. His first game back was at home to Queens Park Rangers, and he scored the winning goal just before the hour in a 2-1 victory. Lester would go on to play for Forest for another two seasons, interrupted by a knee ligament injury, until he was released for a second time at the end of the 2006/07 season.

SATURDAY 5th DECEMBER 1970

Further question marks were raised over Matt Gillies' abilities in the hot-seat at the club after an appalling display at Southampton which saw the club go down 4-1. It was Forest's sixth successive league defeat – indeed, the club had managed to gather only a single point since the sale of Henry Newton nearly two months previously. Peter Cormack, pressed into the centre forward role following Gillies signing Alex Ingram's tally of zero goals in 12 games, got Forest's consolation. Ron Davies (2), Brian O'Neil and Tom Jenkins netted for the Saints.

SATURDAY 5th DECEMBER 1992

Bottom-placed Forest were the weekend's most unexpected winners, triumphing 4-1 at Elland Road. It was the first time Leeds United, the current champions, had lost at home since April 13th 1991. Roy Keane scored twice for Forest, with the other goals coming from Nigel Clough and Kingsley Black.

SATURDAY 6th DECEMBER 1980

There was an unfamiliar name wearing the number 11 shirt for Forest in a home match against Crystal Palace – 18-year-old midfielder Colin Walsh, who'd only made his debut a week previously as a sub for the injured John Robertson. Robertson's absence brought to a halt a run of 243 consecutive appearances by the Scottish left-wing maestro, who had last missed a match almost four years beforehand. Walsh scored on his full debut, hitting the second goal in a 3-0 Forest victory. The others came from a Frank Gray penalty and a Peter Ward effort.

SATURDAY 7th DECEMBER 1938

Forest suffered their heaviest defeat for two seasons, going down 7-1 to Chesterfield at Saltergate, with inside-forward Tom Lyon scoring four goals.

THURSDAY 7th DECEMBER 1978

Resigned to the fact that his number one transfer target, Birmingham City's Trevor Francis, may cost the club too much, Brian Clough settled instead for Derby County's maverick forward Charlie George. The Derby board instantly knocked back any bids, claiming that the loss of George would decrease Derby's attendances and increase Forest's. George would eventually join Forest on loan from Southampton in 1980, staying for a month.

SATURDAY 8th DECEMBER 1984

A tremendous fight-back from the Reds saw them recover from two first-half goals from Gordon Strachan to beat Manchester United 3-2 at the City Ground. Steve Hodge pulled a goal back on 63, Gary Mills equalised on 78 and Johnny Metgod won it with a last minute curling free kick.

SATURDAY 9th DECEMBER 1978

Forest's long, record-breaking run came to an end with a 2-0 defeat by Liverpool at Anfield. Terry McDermott scored a penalty after half an hour and, with Forest being constantly thwarted in their quest for an equaliser, McDermott struck a second time four minutes into the second half to provide his team with an unassailable lead. Forty-two league games undefeated would remain a record until it was surpassed by Arsene Wenger's Arsenal side in August 2004, who would then go on to set a new record of 49.

SATURDAY 9th DECEMBER 2000

David Platt used his contacts at Arsenal to secure the signing on loan of future England international Matthew Upson, but the highly promising youngster had one of the shortest Forest careers of all time, lasting just 85 minutes. He made his debut in midfield in a neat 2-0 win over Portsmouth at the City Ground, but was injured and substituted with five minutes to go. The injury was serious enough to curtail his move as he was sent back to Highbury.

SATURDAY 10th DECEMBER 1977

The first threat to Forest's team harmony came during a 2-1 win over Coventry City at the City Ground, when rugged centre-back Larry Lloyd hobbled off the pitch at the end of the game complaining of a pain in his foot. An examination revealed a broken toe and Lloyd was ruled out for up to two months, eventually being restricted to just seven more league games that season. Clough immediately moved into the transfer market, snapping up ex-Notts County defender David Needham from Queens Park Rangers for £140,000.

MONDAY 10th DECEMBER 1979

Brian Clough made his second attempt to replace Archie Gemmill as Forest's midfield engine following the stark failure of Asa Hartford, signing Queens Park Rangers playmaker Stan Bowles. This move turned out not to be quite as unsuccessful as Hartford's, as the unpredictable Bowles would at least play more than three games for the club, but issues over Clough's training methods and being forced to play on the right of midfield after a career orchestrating play from the centre made this an unhappy period in Bowles' career.

SATURDAY 11th DECEMBER 1976

Forest's 'Battle of the Promising Keepers' was over. John Middleton kept a clean sheet in a 2-0 win away at Millwall, and Peter Wells, who had begun the season in possession of the number one jersey, was sold to Southampton. Wells would play five seasons in the top flight for the Saints before being replaced by a certain Peter Shilton, moving on to Millwall and then Leyton Orient.

SATURDAY 11th DECEMBER 2004

The bad news: Bottom-placed Nottingham Forest lost their latest league game, 3-0, away from home. The really bad news: Their opponents were deadly rivals Derby County, who sealed an easy win thanks to an early Tommy Smith strike and two goals from Grzegorz Rasiak. The good news: It's Joe Kinnear's last game in charge.

THURSDAY 12th DECEMBER 1968

Matt Gillies announced the capture of Derry City's promising young defender Billy O'Kane. 'Billy' would eventually become known as Liam, taking over first from Terry Hennessey as centre-back, then Peter Hindley at right-back, before injury ended his playing career in 1976.

TUESDAY 12th DECEMBER 2006

Salisbury City came to the City Ground for an FA Cup second round replay buoyed by holding Forest to a 1-1 draw nine days previously, and were good value for another stalemate until poor finishing cost them. Nathan Tyson broke the deadlock on 53 after being cleverly fed by 'Junior' Agogo, then with just under ten to go an offside-looking Tyson was allowed to go forward to feed Nicky Southall with a simple goal.

MONDAY 13th DECEMBER 1976

Forest had an unnecessary interruption to their promotion campaign in being forced to play the two-legged final of the Anglo-Scottish Cup over three days in midweek, making it four games in eight days. They took on Leyton Orient at Brisbane Road, where a John Robertson goal secured a 1-1 draw.

SATURDAY 13th DECEMBER 1987

Nigel Clough set a record for the quickest top-flight hat-trick in a 4-0 City Ground victory over Queens Park Rangers, scoring three goals in four minutes. Tommy Gaynor had given Forest the lead three minutes before the break, and an edgy contest was moving into the last ten when Clough scored his first on 81, then his second on 83. Ninety seconds later Forest were awarded a penalty and Clough stepped up to complete his record-breaking hat-trick, blasting the ball past David Seaman.

THURSDAY 14th DECEMBER 1967

Ian Woan was born in Heswall, Cheshire. One of Brian Clough's unearthed non-league diamonds, Woan was signed from Runcorn for a generous £80,000 in March 1990, appearing in the reserves for a while before being given his chance on the left of midfield at the tail end of the 1990/91 season. The languid winger impressed enough to keep his place right up to and including the 1991 FA Cup final. Woan spent a decade at the City Ground, and became noted for his elegant passing, fierce shooting and expertise at dead ball situations. His pinnacle moment came in an FA Cup tie at home to Tottenham in February 1996 when he crashed two superlative free kicks past the England goalkeeper Ian Walker. Woan was released at the end of the 1999/2000 season, and went on to play for Barnsley, Swindon Town, Shrewsbury Town and a handful of teams in the USA. He had a brief spell as caretaker manager of Portsmouth in 2009 before reverting back to a coaching role there.

TUESDAY 14th DECEMBER 2010

Billy Davies' latest attempt to secure a replacement for the injured Dexter Blackstock was knocked back when Millwall rejected a £2 million bid for striker Steve Morison.

SATURDAY 15th DECEMBER 1894

Nottingham Forest turned up for a First Division game at Sheffield Wednesday minus a goalkeeper, as custodian Dan Allsop was unexpectedly absent. Centre forward Thomas Rose went in between the posts instead and kept a clean sheet in a 0-0 draw. It later transpired that Allsop had missed his train to Sheffield.

WEDNESDAY 15th DECEMBER 1976

Brian Clough won his first piece of silverware as Forest boss as the Reds completed a 5-1 aggregate victory over Leyton Orient in the final of the Anglo-Scottish Cup. The scorers for Forest were Colin Barrett (2), 'Sammy' Chapman and Ian Bowyer. Forest: Middleton, Anderson, Clark, McGovern, Lloyd, Chapman, O'Neill, Barrett, Bowery, Bowyer, Robertson. John O'Hare, Tony Woodcock and Peter Withe had played in the first leg instead of Chapman, Barrett and Bowery, with Barrett coming on as a sub for Withe.

MONDAY 16th DECEMBER 1985

The powers that be behind the Irish national team formally requested permission to interview Brian Clough for the job of manager, available after the resignation of Eoin Hand. The Forest board of directors refused, and the job eventually went to Jack Charlton, who would go on to guide Ireland through their greatest period of international success.

THURSDAY 16th DECEMBER 2004

Christmas came nine days early for several thousand Forest supporters when Joe Kinnear tendered his resignation as boss after barely ten months in charge. Forest were unable to continue the impetus that Kinnear's appointment had given the side after Paul Hart's departure, and there were rumours about the squad's lack of fitness and Kinnear's prehistoric training techniques. The club's position of 22nd in the second flight simply was not good enough, and a 3-0 defeat at Derby County came as the final straw. Kinnear would remain out of work for almost four years until he took over at Newcastle United, staying at St James' Park until ill health forced him to hand over the reins to Chris Hughton in February 2009.

SATURDAY 17th DECEMBER 1977

The game in which the realistic nature of Nottingham Forest's campaign to win the First Division title finally came to everyone's notice. The Reds travelled to Old Trafford and trounced Tommy Docherty's Manchester United side 4-0, with goals from Tony Woodcock (2), John Robertson and a Brian Greenhoff own goal. Forest could have doubled that tally, and Clough was later critical of the side's finishing, particularly that of Peter Withe.

WEDNESDAY 17th DECEMBER 1980

The Reds lost their grip on one European trophy, losing 1-0 to Valencia at the Luís Casanova Stadium in the European Super Cup. A Fernando Morena effort on 51 was enough to see the Spanish side triumph on the away goals. Forest: Shilton, Anderson, Gunn, McGovern, Lloyd, Burns, O'Neill, Ponte, Francis, Wallace, Walsh.

FRIDAY 17th DECEMBER 1982

The unhappy footballing marriage between Brian Clough and Justin Fashanu was finally granted a divorce as the young striker was sold across the river to Notts County for £150,000 – £850,000 less than the amount he had cost the club in the summer of 1981.

THURSDAY 18th DECEMBER 1975

Brian Clough continued his cull of players he didn't fancy at his latest club by selling popular midfielder George Lyall to Hull City. Lyall had slipped down the pecking order at Forest behind recent recruit Terry Curran and the re-emerging Martin O'Neill, and so saw a move as his only realistic option in his quest for first-team action. He played for the Tigers for two seasons before moving into non-league with Scarborough.

SATURDAY 18th DECEMBER 2010

Loan signing Marcus Tudgay marked his Forest debut with a goal a minute into the second half of a 3-0 home league victory against Crystal Palace. Tudgay became an instant hero eleven days later by scoring a brace in a 5-2 victory over his former club, Derby County, and earned himself a permanent transfer from Sheffield Wednesday for £500,000 in the process. He ended the season with a satisfactory seven goals from 22 games.

SATURDAY 19th DECEMBER 1903

A shocking, uncharacteristic home performance by Nottingham Forest saw them beaten 7-3 by Aston Villa at the City Ground, their only excuse being the loss of left-back Jim Iremonger early in the game. Tommy Niblo, who would join Forest at the end of the season, and Joe Bache both scored hat-tricks for the Villans. The Forest scorers were Grenville Morris (2) and Billy Shearman.

THURSDAY 19th DECEMBER 1996

Frank Clark tendered his resignation as Forest manager after three and a half years in charge, two days after losing 4-2 at Liverpool, admitting that he thought himself unable to turn things around. The loss at Anfield was the Reds' 16th game without a win, and they'd been bottom of the Premiership for a month. This was a sad end to Clark's time at the helm, coming after promotion, a third place finish in the top flight and reaching the quarter-finals of the UEFA Cup. If the £8.5 million generated by the sale of Stan Collymore had been spent on better players than Chris Bart-Williams, Kevin Campbell and the dreadful Andrea Silenzi, things may have turned out considerably differently.

FRIDAY 20th DECEMBER 1968

The City Ground hosted an Under-23 match between England and Italy. No Forest players made the team (the last Forest player to be picked for the England U23 side was Henry Newton, 18 months previously). England ran out 1-0 winners thanks to a goal from Southampton's Martin Chivers.

FRIDAY 20th DECEMBER 1996

There was a surprise appointment as Frank Clark's temporary successor in the Forest hot-seat – the club's left-back, Stuart Pearce. 'Psycho' immediately began plotting the downfall of his first opponents in management, George Graham's second-placed Arsenal...

SATURDAY 21st DECEMBER 1996

...which he achieved with a come-from-behind 2-1 win. Infamously, Pearce made his first ever team selection by writing down all the names of his first-team squad on pieces of paper and then arranging them into a 4-5-2 he was satisfied with...until his wife pointed out he'd neglected to select a goalkeeper. Pearce recalled Brian Roy and Nikola Jerkan and it was the latter who had the greatest impact on the game. An argument with Gunner Ian Wright ended with Wright elbowing Jerkan and getting sent off. Wright had given Arsenal the lead after 67 minutes, but two goals from Alf-Inge Håland – the second in the last minute – gave Pearce a winning start.

FOREST'S SECOND-HIGHEST SCORER ALL OF TIME, NIGEL CLOUGH, MADE HIS DEBUT FOR FOREST AGAINST WATFORD ON BOXING DAY, 1984.

SATURDAY 22nd DECEMBER 1979

The worrying dip in Forest's form continued with a 3-0 defeat at Old Trafford, meaning Brian Clough's side hadn't won a single league game for seven weeks. The addition of Stan Bowles for his debut had little to no effect, as goals by Joe Jordan (2) and Gordon McQueen sent Forest crashing to their seventh defeat in ten games.

SATURDAY 22nd DECEMBER 1990

Brian Clough took his surprisingly mid-table Forest side up to Sheffield to take on Dave Bassett's Sheffield United. The Blades hadn't won a single league game so far that season, so – typically – Forest lost, despite at one stage leading through goals by Roy Keane and Stuart Pearce in answer to Ian Bryson's opener. Bryson again and Brian Deane secured their manager a 3-2 victory. This would start a marked revival for United, who went on to win ten of their next 13 games and finish in a creditable 13th place.

SATURDAY 23rd DECEMBER 1933

Tom Peacock scored four goals for Forest in a 6-1 win over Port Vale at the City Ground, the other goals coming from Johnny Dent and Harry Race. Peacock would score four goals in a game no less than four times in his Forest career, twice against the unfortunate Valiants.

THURSDAY 23rd DECEMBER 2010

Billy Davies announced the capture of Portland Timbers striker-winger Robbie Finlay, using his family ties, as the manager of Timbers was the former Rangers and Chelsea forward John Spencer, who also happened to be Davies' brother-in-law. Finlay had an unfortunate start to his Forest career, being injured in his first training session and hence sidelined until April.

SATURDAY 24th DECEMBER 1910

Centre-half Joe Mercer made his debut in a game at home to Tottenham Hotspur. Joe's son, also called Joe, would go on to play more than 400 games for Everton and Arsenal, as well as taking temporary change of the England national side in 1974.

SATURDAY 24th DECEMBER 1954

Forest made one of their most successful signings of all time by forking out a hefty fee for West Ham United striker Jim Barrett. Barrett would go on to score a marvellous 69 goals for the club in only 117 games, helping Forest back up to the top flight in 1957.

TUESDAY 25th DECEMBER 1900

Bolton Wanderers were forced to put reserve forward Jimmy Hanson in goal in a league game at Forest after regular keeper John Sutcliffe broke a finger in the pre-match kickabout. The Reds took full advantage of the Trotters' misfortune and won 3-0 thanks to goals from Grenville Morris and Fred Forman (2).

TUESDAY 25th DECEMBER 1951

A massive holiday crowd of 61,062 attended the 11am fixture at Hillsborough between Forest and Sheffield Wednesday. What made this huge figure more impressive was the fact that in those days there was no public transport on Christmas Day, and as only the quite affluent at the time could afford a car, the majority of those in attendance had travelled to Hillsborough on foot. The game ended all square, Noel Kelly scoring for Forest and Walter Rickett for the Owls.

FRIDAY 26th DECEMBER 1924

During a league game at home to Bolton Wanderers, Forest were awarded a penalty which, as the regular penalty taker, Harry Martin, was currently off the field of play receiving treatment for an injury, no-one else on the Forest side seemed to have the nerve to take. Martin was therefore carried from the dressing room to the penalty spot, where he swung a boot at the ball and scored, before collapsing and being carried back off the pitch. Forest drew the game 1-1.

FRIDAY 26th DECEMBER 1952

Wally Ardron returned from a one-match rest and scored all four in a 4-1 home win over Hull City, recording the 200th league goal of his career in the process. Ardron scored with two headers in the 7th and 39th minutes and two shots on 39 and 65. Danish international Viggo Jensen scored Hull's consolation effort from the spot on 67.

WEDNESDAY 26th DECEMBER 1984

The 18-year-old Nigel Clough received a late Christmas present from his dad, who handed him a league debut for Forest in a home game against Ipswich Town, which the Reds won 2-0 thanks to goals by Steve Hodge and Johnny Metgod. Clough Junior's debut came 22 years to the day since the injury which ended Clough Senior's playing career, during a match between Bury and Sunderland.

THURSDAY 26th DECEMBER 1991

Nigel Clough celebrated the seventh anniversary of that league debut in the correct way, by scoring after 11 minutes at White Hart Lane in a league game. It all went wrong seven minutes from time when, as the game descended into slight ugliness, Clough was given his marching orders by Ray Biggar for hacking down Paul Stewart, who had equalised for Spurs just before the hour. The last laugh was Forest's, though, as a typically unstoppable Stuart Pearce free kick three minutes into injury time sent them home victorious.

FRIDAY 26th DECEMBER 2008

Reds manager Colin Calderwood had his festive cheer dampened by the news that he was out of work. Having finally guided Forest out of the third tier the previous season, they looked likely to be heading straight back down having won just four games so far this term, spending the entire season in the relegation zone. The latest reverse – a 4-2 home defeat by Doncaster Rovers in which Rovers had at one stage been 4-0 up – was the final straw for hairman Nigel Doughty, and Calderwood was informed his services were no longer required.

MONDAY 27th DECEMBER 1971

There was a rare moment of sunshine in an otherwise dreadful season for the Forest support when, in a league game at home to Arsenal, left-winger Ian Storey-Moore scored the best goal of his career. He received the ball just outside Forest's penalty area, ran 74 yards to leave several Arsenal players (including Alan Ball making his Gunners debut) bemused and a couple on their backsides, and then coolly rounded the keeper and slotted the ball home.

THURSDAY 27th DECEMBER 2012

Forest supporters still reeling from Sean O'Driscoll's shock sacking as manager on Boxing Day after a 4-2 home win against Leeds United, are further shocked when ex-Scotland boss Alex McLeish is installed as manager. McLeish would only last 40 days in the hot-seat, during which club ambassador Frank Clark, chief executive Mark Arthur and head of recruitment Keith Burt were all also dismissed, before leaving "by mutual consent". McLeish only won one and lost five of his seven games in charge.

WEDNESDAY 28th DECEMBER 1977

Nottingham Forest's latest victory – a 2-0 win at failing Newcastle United thanks to goals by David Needham and John McGovern – saw them edge five points clear at the top of the First Division table. 'The last time Nottingham were five ahead of anyone was in a cricket match,' quipped Brian Clough. 'Obviously I am delighted. Peter Taylor and I never enjoyed such a lead while we were winning the league title with Derby County.'

SUNDAY 28th DECEMBER 1986

Ian Bowyer scored the 100th goal of his lengthy career, a last minute thunderbolt to secure a point in a 2-2 home draw with Luton Town.

WEDNESDAY 29th DECEMBER 1915

One of the greatest servants in Forest's history, Bob McCall, was born in Worksop. His playing career at the club stretched for 16 seasons. He lost eight seasons due to World War II, playing less than 200 games for Forest – most of them at left-back.

WEDNESDAY 29th DECEMBER 2010

Nothing perhaps satisfies a Forest supporter more than a comfortable victory over Derby County, and tonight's 5-2 victory for the Reds over the Rams sent the majority of the City Ground home with huge smiles on their faces. Even more satisfying was the fact that four of the goals came from ex-Derby players – Rob Earnshaw and Marcus Tudgay with two goals apiece. Luke Chambers completed matters.

SATURDAY 30th DECEMBER 1989

Brian Clough celebrated his 1,000th league game as a football manager by sending out a team to succeed in doing what he sent out a team to do for the previous 999 – win it. White Hart Lane was the venue and the opponents, appropriately, were Tottenham Hotspur, Clough's first ever opponents as Forest manager. Despite Gary Lineker giving Tottenham an 11th-minute lead, an inspired Forest were on top form and goals by Nigel Clough, Gary Crosby and Garry Parker gave the Reds an unassailable 3-1 advantage. Even Lineker's last minute tap-in to make it 3-2 failed to spoil Old Big Ed's perfect day.

TUESDAY 30th DECEMBER 2008

The bookies installed Billy Davies as the favourite to take over as Forest's next manager following the Boxing Day dismissal of Colin Calderwood. Some priced the ex-Derby boss at 2/5, with Burton Albion manager Nigel Clough the next-best priced at 8/1 (although Clough was also the 2/1 favourite to be named the next manager of Derby County). Also in the frame, allegedly, were Aidy Boothroyd (9/1), Alan Curbishley (14/1) and Roy Keane (16/1).

SATURDAY 31st DECEMBER 1960

1960 ended unexpectedly dismally for Forest, with a 5-3 home defeat to Arsenal. This reversal in their fortunes came as a surprise as they had won seven and drawn two of their previous nine games, coming after a run of seven consecutive league defeats. It was also the first time rookie keeper Peter Grummitt had been on the losing side since making his debut almost two months before. Forest's goals came from Johnny Quigley (2) and a Calvin Palmer penalty. David Herd scored a hat-trick for the Gunners.

SATURDAY 31st DECEMBER 1988

Neil Webb scored the 100th league goal of his career, playing for Forest against Sheffield Wednesday at Hillsborough. He scored the middle goal of three as the Reds triumphed 3-0, the other goals coming from Tommy Gaynor and Steve Hodge. It was a remarkable achievement for Webb, who was still only 25 and had played the entirety of his career until then as a midfielder.